Maryland
HSA Finish Line
English 10

Continental Press

Credits:

Acknowledgments: Page 7, "One Day," and Pages 27–29: "At the Fair" by Leslie Hall, copyright © Leslie Hall. Used by permission.

Photo Credits: Front cover and title page: Courtesy of National Park Service; Page 51: Library of Congress, Prints and Photographs Division, LC-USZ62-132047

ISBN 0-8454-4901-X

Copyright © 2006 The Continental Press, Inc.

No part of this publication may be reproduced in any form or by any means, electronic, mechanical, photocopying, recording, or otherwise, without the prior written permission of the publisher. All rights reserved. Printed in the United States of America.

CONTENTS

The Maryland High School Assessment for English covers Maryland's Core Learning Goals and includes material generally taught in a full-year English course. To help you prepare for the test, each of the four units in this workbook is devoted to one of the Core Learning Goals.

- Unit 1, **Responding to a Text,** relates to Goal 1:
"The student will demonstrate the ability to respond to a text by employing personal experiences and critical analysis."

- Unit 2, **Writing Compositions,** relates to Goal 2:
"The student will demonstrate the ability to compose in a variety of modes by developing content, employing specific forms, and selecting language appropriate for a particular audience and purpose."

- Unit 3, **Using Language,** relates to Goal 3:
"The student will demonstrate the ability to control language by applying the conventions of Standard English in writing and speaking."

- Unit 4, **Evaluating Text,** relates to Goal 4:
"The student will demonstrate the ability to evaluate the content, organization, and language use of texts."

Under each goal, there are numbered Expectations and Indicators. In this workbook, each lesson is devoted to one or more of these Indicators, which appear in colored boxes in the introduction of the lesson. For example, on page 6 you will see the following Indicator, with an explanation below it:

1.1.1 The student will use pre-reading strategies appropriate to both the text and purpose for reading by surveying the text, accessing prior knowledge, formulating questions, setting purpose(s), and making predictions.

After the lesson introduction of the skills, there is **Guided Practice.** In this section, you will read a selection and answer questions. After each question, you will find an explanation of the correct answer in a shaded box. So you will answer questions and find out right away if you are right. You will also learn *why* one answer is right and the others are not. Following the Guided Practice is a section called **Test Yourself,** where you will read selections and answer questions on your own to check your mastery of the skill.

© The Continental Press, Inc.   Do not duplicate.

Most of the questions are multiple-choice questions, a format which is probably familiar to you. The answer choices alternate ABCD and FGHJ. There are also Brief Constructed-Response **(BCR)** questions and essay questions (Extended Constructed-Response, or **ECR).** The essay questions are found in Unit 2, Writing Compositions. Rather than Guided Practice and Test Yourself, in many of these lessons you will be guided through instruction and exercises related to writing an essay. Unit 3, Lesson 3 (Capitalization, Punctuation, and Spelling) also has a different format, with practice exercises interspersed with instruction and review instead of separate Guided Practice and Test Yourself sections.

When you finish this book, you'll be ready for the Maryland High School Assessment for English. Good luck!

© The Continental Press, Inc.   Do not duplicate.

RESPONDING TO A TEXT

You may think you do not read very much, but every day you use many different kinds of reading skills—the same skills that you need for a test. You read labels on things you might want to buy, you read directions when you use a machine or tool, you read the computer screen while you are surfing the Internet or exchanging e-mails, and, of course, you read books, magazines, and tests.

As you read, you respond to the text in different ways. Most of the time, this process is automatic, and not something you do consciously. In your mind, you ask yourself questions about the things you read. The goal of Unit 1 is that you will be able to show that you can respond to text (things you read) by using your personal experience, and by critical analysis (asking questions and thinking about the meaning of what you read.)

Lesson 1

Reading Strategies

No matter what you read, you use strategies that you may not even be aware of. You use these reading strategies before you read, while you are reading, and after you read. When you are taking a test, think about the reading strategies and use them; they will help you improve your score.

1.1.1 The student will use pre-reading strategies appropriate to both the text and purpose for reading by surveying the text, accessing prior knowledge, formulating questions, setting purpose(s), and making predictions.

Before You Read

There are several strategies that will help you prepare to read a passage. Before you read:

- **Survey,** or skim, what you are going to read. Look at the whole article, story, or poem. Read the title and look for subheads, pictures, captions, and other aids that give you information.

- Ask yourself what you already know about the topic. Suppose you have to read a passage with the title "Wild Horses of Assateague." Think about what

© The Continental Press, Inc.   Do not duplicate.

and where Assateague is first. You probably know that it is an island off the coast of Maryland and Virginia. The things you already know about the topic are your **prior knowledge.**

- Then you might ask yourself what wild horses have to do with an island. That's a **question** you want to answer, and it is part of your **purpose** for reading the passage. When you finish reading it, you should have your answer—and be able to answer questions about the passage.

- **Predict** what you think the article will be about. The title gives you a good idea of topic and will start you thinking about what the author will say. You will probably revise your prediction as you go along and get more information.

Guided Practice

Read the following poem and answer the questions.

> In 1963, Reverend Martin Luther King, Jr., gave his famous "I Have a Dream" speech, in which he spoke eloquently of the day when racial equality would be a fact of life in the United States. Almost 100 years earlier, Elizabeth Cady Stanton, Susan B. Anthony, and many others worked for women's suffrage under the slogan, "Not for ourselves alone."

One Day

Never forget that one day
a brave man stood up for all of us.
He said, "I have a dream,"
and his dream flew around the country
on beating wings,
stirring the winds of change.

Never forget that one day
those brave women stood up for all of us.
They said, "Not for ourselves alone,"
and their words rang out
like the bell of freedom,
tolling for equality.

Never forget that one day
each act was once only a word,
each word was once only a whisper,
each whisper was once only a dream.

by Leslie Hall

© The Continental Press, Inc.   Do not duplicate.

Which topic would be <u>most</u> helpful to discuss to prepare for reading the poem?

    A winged animals   **C** the revolutionary war

    B symbols in dreams   **D** the civil rights movement

First, think about the main theme of the poem. The poem is about freedom, but you can eliminate C because it is not about the revolutionary war. Although the poem does refer to wings and dreams, you can tell that A and B are not the most likely answers because the poem is more concerned with racial equality and women's voting rights. Choice D fits best.

After previewing the paragraph of background information and the title of the poem, the reader would <u>most likely</u> predict that the poem will

    F describe the speech by Martin Luther King, Jr.

    G teach facts about the life of Elizabeth Cady Stanton

    H tell about injustices that different people have suffered

    J focus on specific times when people fought for their rights

When you preview the poem's title and paragraph of background information before the poem, you can tell that F and G are probably not the best choices. Choice H seems like a possible answer, since the background information describes two groups of people who were denied rights and treated unjustly. However, when you look at choice J, you realize that "One Day" probably refers to a specific time, and it makes sense that the specific time is "when people fought for their rights." Choice J is the best answer.

1.1.2 The student will use during-reading strategies appropriate to both the text and purpose for reading by visualizing, making connections, and using fix-up strategies such as rereading, questioning, and summarizing.

While You Read

Be an active reader. Think about what you are reading. Reread the passage to understand some things you might have missed the first time. Here are some questions to ask yourself while you read:

- What is the **main idea** of the article? Or, what is the **theme** or **lesson** of the story? How can I **summarize** it in one or two sentences?

- What are the story **characters** like? What is the **setting?** Can I picture the **characters** and **setting** in my mind?

- What do I think is likely to **happen next?**

© The Continental Press, Inc.   Do not duplicate.

- When I see an unfamiliar word, what clues can I find to help me figure out the **meaning** of the word?

- How do the events of the story relate to my life and **what I already know?** How does the main idea of the article connect to **what I already know** about the subject?

Guided Practice

Answer these questions about the poem, "One Day."

Which of these best summarizes what happens in the poem?
- **A** A group of women ring a bell together.
- **B** A man dreams about flying around the country.
- **C** Brave people work to make dreams come true.
- **D** Different people learn to speak up for themselves.

When you summarize, you tell the main idea or the main events that happen. Look at all the answer choices. Only choices C and D are possible summaries of the poem. Although the poem does refer to people speaking up for themselves, that is not the main idea of the poem. Reread the last few lines of the poem. You can see that the poem is about the efforts of a few people to act on what was "once only a dream." Choice C is the best answer.

Which of these issues is most like the issues that are discussed in the poem?
- **F** crime rates
- **H** low-cost health insurance
- **G** fairness in the workplace
- **J** welfare assistance

When you read, it is helpful to make connections between what you are reading and what you already know. Look at the list of issues. Then think about the poem. The poem is about struggles for rights and equality. Choice G is about people being treated fairly at work, so it is the only answer that fits.

Unit 1 Responding to a Text

9

© The Continental Press, Inc.   Do not duplicate.

After You Read

After you finish reading, stop and think about what you have read and your purpose for reading. If you were reading to learn something, you'll want to review the facts. You may need to go back and reread some parts of the article to make sure you understood what you read.

Ask yourself some questions like these:

- What do I know after reading this article or story?

- How is this article similar to or different from other materials I have read about this subject?

- How is the new information in this article connected to what I already know about this subject?

- Now that I have read this article or story, what new conclusions can I draw?

It might also help to review the information by organizing the facts in a chart or another kind of graphic organizer. You could write notes to summarize what you read. Writing about what you have read can also help you remember it.

Guided Practice

Now answer two more questions about the poem, "One Day."

After reading the poem, which of these conclusions may be drawn?
   A   Hard work usually pays off.
   B   It takes many people to fight injustice.
   C   Great changes may begin with a dream.
   D   People must speak loudly in order to be heard.

Think about the main theme of the poem. Then look again at the answer choices. You can eliminate choice A because it is not really related to the theme. You can also eliminate choices B and D, because these messages are not found in the poem. Choice C is the best answer.

© The Continental Press, Inc.   Do not duplicate.

Which of these proverbs <u>best</u> relates to the theme of this poem?

    F "Pride goes before a fall."

    G "A rolling stone gathers no moss."

    H "People who live in glass houses should not throw stones."

    J "A journey of a thousand miles begins with a single step."

> Look at the answer choices as you think about the poem. Which proverb best describes the theme of the struggles for civil rights and voting rights? These struggles may be considered overwhelming, like a long journey. However, when one person is brave enough to face the obstacles, the journey has begun with that "single step." Choice J is the best answer.

Test Yourself

Read the article "Jazz Improvisation." Then answer Numbers 1 through 6.

Jazz Improvisation
by Sally Johnston

Jazz music can be played by many different instruments. Some jazz is seamless and predictable, while other jazz is spirited and full of surprises. The one ingredient almost all jazz shares is improvisation.

When a musician improvises, he or she is composing and performing at the same time. Improvisation is usually the culmination of a jazz performance. However, the process is not simple. Even though jazz musicians create their music as they go along, improvisation is still an art that takes years of hard work and practice.

One jazz musician uses three words to describe the creative process of improvisation: imitation, assimilation, and innovation. Musicians imitate by listening to other musicians for ideas and then playing what they hear. Next, they assimilate the music and begin to understand it. Finally, they are ready to innovate and create new music.

Learning jazz can be compared to learning how to speak. When we first start talking, we learn by listening to others and imitating them. Then we begin to speak on our own. We learn to form our own thoughts into words and phrases. Eventually, we reach the point where we know what we want to say and how to say it. This is similar to the jazz musician's progress from listening, to practicing, to creating.

Preparing to be a successful jazz musician is very demanding. Just as it takes people years to develop language skills, it takes a jazz musician years to develop improvisational skills.

© The Continental Press, Inc.   Do not duplicate.

Many jazz musicians never improvise in the same way twice. This requires them to continually develop new and innovative combinations of notes and instruments. In one recording session, for instance, the same song might be played in several different ways. This variety keeps jazz lively.

Jazz musicians often start with a tune they all know. They play the tune the entire way through with the horns playing the melody and the piano, bass, and drums playing the accompaniment. The second time through, the piano, bass, and drums play the same tune, but the horn players begin to improvise. People who are not familiar with jazz can't always tell when the musicians are improvising. If a section of a performance sounds improvised, it probably is.

Not all jazz is improvised, and most jazz bands do practice some arrangements for each show. You can tell when someone in a large band is improvising because the soloist will stand while playing.

The next time you go to a jazz performance, lend an ear to improvisation.

1 **After previewing the title and the first paragraph of "Jazz Improvisation," a reader would predict that most jazz music**

   A   is familiar to the audience

   B   is predictable to the audience

   C   sounds like speech when it is played

   D   sounds different each time it is played

2 **Which of these topics would be most helpful to discuss when preparing to read the article?**

   F   the history of jazz

   G   how people get ideas

   H   where jazz is played

   J   how people learn speech

3 **Which of these is most like a jazz musician who is improvising?**

   A   A singer sings a song as it was arranged by the songwriter.

   B   An author writes a story about an event that actually happened.

   C   A sculptor makes a statue that looks exactly like the model who is posing.

   D   An artist creates a painting that blends elements of reality and imagination.

© The Continental Press, Inc.   Do not duplicate.

4 **Which conclusion may be drawn from the information in the article?**

    F Jazz is fairly easy for beginners to master.

    G Musicians who play jazz are skilled and creative.

    H Jazz bands prefer to play music that is pre-arranged.

    J A person who speaks well will be able to learn jazz.

5 **What evidence from the article supports the idea that "preparing to be a jazz musician is very demanding"?**

    A Learning to play music is similar to learning how to speak.

    B It takes many years to develop the skills needed to improvise.

    C Jazz bands practice some music that has already been arranged.

    D Jazz music can be predictable, or it can be spirited and surprising.

6 **Which of the following best summarizes this article?**

    F Jazz music can be played by many different instruments. Some jazz is seamless and predictable, while other jazz is spirited and full of surprises.

    G Learning music is like learning to talk. When we first start talking, we learn by listening to others and imitating them. Then we begin to speak on our own, forming thoughts into words and phrases. Finally, we know what we want to say and how to say it.

    H Improvisation is not always noticed by people who are unfamiliar with jazz. If a section sounds improvised, it probably is. But this does not mean that all jazz is improvised.

    J Improvisation is an important part of jazz music. Learning to improvise takes years of study. When jazz musicians improvise, they imitate a piece of music, then they understand the music, and finally, they create a new version of the music. Improvisation helps keep jazz lively.

© The Continental Press, Inc.   Do not duplicate.

Lesson 2

Genre and Structure

You have probably read many literary passages for school assignments and even just for fun. Some examples of literary passages include poems, plays, stories, novels, and essays. Each of these genres, or forms of literature, has an identifiable structure and characteristics that help readers know whether they are reading a poem, a play, a story, or another kind of literature. The structure of a work of literature helps give the passage form and meaning. This, in turn, helps you understand what you read.

Unlike most informational reading passages, which explain how to do something or tell about a thing or event, literary reading passages often have layers of meaning. A poem might describe an event or an object that symbolizes an idea. In addition, the poet most likely uses structures such as a particular rhythm, a rhyme scheme, or specific words and phrases to give readers certain feelings when they read the poem.

This lesson focuses on the genre and structure of poetry. You will read other genres of literature in the rest of this book.

1.1.5 The student will identify specific structural elements of particular literary forms: poetry, short story, novel, drama, essay, biography, autobiography, journalistic writing, and film.

Literary Genre and Structure

This indicator focuses on identifying different genres or forms of literature and their structures. On a test, you may be asked to read a passage and then answer questions about what genre of literature the passage is (poetry, short story, etc.) and the structure or characteristics of the passage.

Here are some terms and definitions you will need to know about various literary genres:

- *autobiography*—nonfiction that an author writes about his or her own life
- *ballad*—a song that tells a story, usually with a tragic ending
- *biography*—nonfiction written about a person's life
- *comedy*—a play written to entertain and amuse
- *couplet*—two rhyming lines that appear one after the other
- *dramatic monologue*—the speech of one person alone in a dramatic work

© The Continental Press, Inc.   Do not duplicate.

- *epic*—a long poem that tells a heroic story
- *essay*—a composition about a certain topic
- *novel*—a book-length work of narrative fiction
- *novella*—a long short story
- *poem*—writing in verse that may be rhymed or may have a certain number of syllables per line
- *short story*—a short work of fiction
- *sonnet*—a poem of fourteen lines, usually in iambic pentameter
- *tragedy*—a play which ends in sorrow for the hero or heroine

The structures or characteristics of different literary genres support the intended purpose. For example, the purpose of both tragedy and comedy is to bring about some kind of emotional response from the reader or audience, but tragedies and comedies are very different from one another. A comedy contains humorous language and situations to make the reader laugh, while a tragedy describes a situation that makes the reader feel the character's suffering or sorrow.

When distinguishing among different literary genres, think about these questions:

- What is the form of this work of literature?
- What is probably the purpose of this writing?
- What does the author want the reader to think or feel?
- How do the different structures of this form of writing support the purpose?

Guided Practice

Read the poem and answer the questions.

What Time Is It?

1   Ticking, tocking, half past ten
        the clanging clock chimes yet again.
    Yet again the hands move round—
        days wind up and days wind down.
5   One day ends and another season begins
        while clock hands continue to spin
        the question of what matters.

© The Continental Press, Inc.   Do not duplicate.

Which of these best describes the form of lines 1 through 6 of the poem?

    A couplets   **C** a refrain

    B an introduction   **D** stanzas

When you look at lines 1–6, you can tell that the lines are in rhyming pairs, or couplets, so choice A is correct.

One way readers can tell this passage is a poem is that it

    F has some words that begin with the same sound

    G uses repetition and figurative language

    H is about how time passes

    J is in rhyming verse

The poem does have some words that begin with the same sound, uses repetition and figurative language, and is about how time passes. But none of these elements are specific to poetry as a form. Choice J is correct because it is the only choice that tells what makes poetry different from other forms of literature—the poem is in rhyming verse.

Test Yourself

Read the poems "The Sky Is Low, the Clouds Are Mean" and "haiku." Then answer Numbers 1 through 3.

The Sky Is Low, the Clouds Are Mean
by Emily Dickinson

The sky is low, the clouds are mean,
A traveling flake of snow
Across a barn or through a rut
Debates if it will go.

A narrow wind complains all day
How someone treated him;
Nature, like us, is sometimes caught
Without her diadem.

haiku
by Onitsura

Cool are the breezes;
The sky's emptiness is filled
With pine-tree voices

© The Continental Press, Inc.   Do not duplicate.

1 A reader can tell that Onitsura's poem is a haiku because it has
    A rhyming words
    B figurative language
    C one stanza with a certain number of words
    D three lines with a certain number of syllables per line

2 Which feature of "The Sky Is Low, the Clouds Are Mean" shows that it is a poem?
    F images of nature as royalty
    G sentences that are long and complex
    H sentences divided into lines and stanzas
    J descriptions of what can be seen in nature

3 "The Sky Is Low, the Clouds Are Mean" has all of these features except
    A rhythm
    B rhyme
    C stanzas
    D couplets

© The Continental Press, Inc.   Do not duplicate.

Lesson 3

Elements of a Narrative

A narrative is any type of story. The story can be written in fictional form (as a short story, a novel, or a novella), as a poem, or as an essay. You have been reading narratives since you first learned to read.

Most narratives have these common elements:

- Setting—where and when the story happens

- Point of view—who tells the story

- Plot—the events or the action of the story

- Characters—the people in the story

- Conflict—struggles or obstacles faced by the people in the story

1.2.1 The student will consider the contributions of plot, character, setting, conflict, and point of view when constructing the meaning of a text.

This indicator focuses on the five elements of a narrative. Questions about this indicator may require you to think about and/or explain how these elements affect and contribute to the meaning of a literary work.

Here are some of the skills that are important in literary reading:

- Analyze characters and what they say.

- Recognize how the characters' words and actions affect the plot.

- Identify the point of view and/or the narrator, and understand how the author's choice of point of view and narrator affects the literary work.

- Identify the setting and consider how the setting affects the overall meaning.

Setting Sometimes the author reveals the setting immediately. There may be a line that describes where the story takes place, such as the following sentence from a story:

> Although Oakdale was only a small Midwestern town, it had the pretensions of a big city.

From this sentence, you can tell that the setting is a small town in the Midwest.

© The Continental Press, Inc.   Do not duplicate.

There may be a sentence that tells the time period or gives a year, like this one:

> Even though skateboarding was practically unknown in 1972, Steve had managed to learn everything there was to know and was already an expert skater.

From this sentence, you can tell that the story takes place in the year 1972.

Even if the setting is not explicitly stated, you can usually figure it out using clues in the reading passage, such as:

- the clothing styles

- the manner of transportation

- the language characters use

- the occupations and leisure activities of the characters

- the presence or absence of different kinds of technology, such as telephones, computers, or the Internet

Point of View

The point of view refers to the person who is telling the story. Who is the author's choice of narrator or speaker? How does this choice affect the tone, the events, and the credibility of the story or poem?

Here are some questions to consider when reading:

- Who is telling the story?

- What can you tell about the narrator from reading the story?

- Is the narrator reliable? Can you believe what the narrator says, or are there contradictions between what the narrator says and what other characters say?

- How does the style of narration affect the story?

The author chooses a narrative style to create a certain tone and support the author's purpose. An author may narrate a story from the first-person point of view (as the "I" character) in order to let the reader feel close to the narrator and to action of the story. This point of view limits what the narrator may discuss, as this character may not be able to determine the unspoken thoughts and motives of other characters. Or, an author may tell a story with the omniscient (or all-knowing) third-person point of view in order to give the reader as much information as possible about the characters and their thoughts and actions. In limited third-person point of view, the narrator is not a character in the story, but the story is narrated from a point of view that is close to that of a particular character.

© The Continental Press, Inc.   Do not duplicate.

Plot

The plot is made up of the events that happen in a story. The author tells the events of the story in a certain order or sequence. Understanding the time and sequence of events in a story helps you understand how one event contributes to another. Authors may use a variety of techniques to present the events of a story, including *flashbacks* and *foreshadowing*:

- *Foreshadowing* is the technique of giving the reader hints about events to come.

- *Flashbacks* interrupt the present moment by describing events from the past.

If the time sequence of a story is complicated, sometimes it is helpful to take notes about which events occur at which point in the story. You could use a graphic organizer like this one:

What happens in the story:		
Beginning	**Middle**	**End**

The main events of the plot are the conflict, action, and resolution.	Usually the main character experiences a problem, confronts conflict, then undergoes some kind of transformation and comes to a resolution of the conflict.

Characters and Conflict

Understanding the plot requires that you also understand who the characters are and what they do and say. Understanding how characters act and how they relate to and communicate with each other is important to understanding the overall meaning of a work of literature. Test questions may ask you to think about characters and their motives (why they do what they do), and then explain how the characters' thoughts, words, and actions influence what happens in a narrative.

Ask yourself these questions to better understand the characters and their contributions to the plot:

- Who are the most important characters?

- Who are the supporting characters?

- How do the characters get along with each other?

- What does each character want?

- What is the main problem or conflict of the story?

- What is the most important action of the story?

© The Continental Press, Inc.   Do not duplicate.

In addition to examining the characters, think about the conflict. Usually, there is a main conflict in a narrative. Sometimes the conflict is a problem or obstacle that the main character faces alone, or sometimes it is a struggle between characters. By the end of the narrative, the main conflict is resolved in some way.

To identify the conflict, first ask what problem the main character faces or what the main conflict is in the narrative. Then think about the resolution. How is the problem solved? What lesson do the characters learn?

It's also helpful to look back at the reading passage to figure out how you know the answers to these questions. Do you get this information from the characters themselves, from other characters, or from the narrator?

Guided Practice

Here is an excerpt from a story about a pioneer family crossing the Rocky Mountains. The story is narrated by a fifteen-year-old girl. Read the excerpt and answer the questions.

> The initial exhilaration and joyful sense of freedom that must accompany any new adventure had been worn away by the combined weight of labor and monotony. Chores that had been accomplished easily at home in the East seemed almost impossible on this journey. Back at home, I would sing as I washed clothes outside in the sunshine, with a washtub next to the well. The clean fragrance of the soap and the sunshine and the sounds of the birds all seemed like a dream to me now as I found myself lugging mounds of soiled clothes across endless fields to the nearest river, almost a mile away.
>
> It seemed to take years to pass the Great Plains, a vast chasm of space filled with dust and heat and boredom. And then, suddenly, without warning, summer was over. Autumn peeked out behind the white clouds in the blue sky, then hid herself again.
>
> Then, just as suddenly, the mountains rose up before us. As we began the climb into the mountains, we could hear the wind whispering, "Hurry, hurry." We could feel the cold breath of winter chasing after us. We could see the clouds gathering snow like soldiers filling ammunition bags.

Which word best describes how the narrator feels?

A weary	**C** eager
B horrified	**D** exhilarated

If you only read the first line of the excerpt, you might think that either choice C or D is true. However, when you read that "it seemed to take years to pass the plains, a vast chasm of space filled with dust and heat and boredom," you know that choice A is correct.

© The Continental Press, Inc.   Do not duplicate.

Which best describes what happens in the excerpt?

    F Children protest forced labor.

    G A soldier prepares for a battle.

    H A girl performs her daily chores.

    J Pioneers face hardships on their travels.

This question is about the plot. Think about what happens in the excerpt. What is the main action? Look in the excerpt for clues. The narrator says they are on a "journey," and that "It seemed to take years to pass the plains." Both these clues hint that the girl is traveling with pioneers going west. The narrator also describes the difficulties of the trip. Choice J is the correct answer.

Where do the events of the excerpt mostly take place?

    A in a city   **C** on the plains

    B in a river   **D** on a battlefield

This question is about the setting. There is no city, so you can eliminate choice A. There is a river in the excerpt, but the action does not take place in the river. When you understand that the "soldiers" are not actually soldiers, and that the girl is traveling "across the plains," you know that choice C is the only answer that fits.

The main conflict in the excerpt is between

    F good and evil   **H** a girl and her family

    G humans and nature   **J** two opposing armies

The excerpt is mostly about one girl's experiences, and not about war or the broad theme of good and evil, so only choice G or H could be correct. Since there is no mention of the girl's family, but the last paragraph does describe the travelers' struggle against the weather, you know that choice G is the right answer.

The story is set in which time period?

    A about 1000 years ago   **C** the present

    B almost 200 years ago   **D** the future

You can eliminate choices C and D because the girl is not using a washing machine, but is washing clothes outside by hand. You may also know that Europeans first traveled to the Americas in the 1400s, and that the pioneers crossed the American plains in the 1800s. Choice B is the correct answer.

© The Continental Press, Inc.   Do not duplicate.

The author's purpose in using the first-person point of view is <u>most likely</u> to

    F   give the reader facts about pioneers

    G   keep the reader interested

    H   help the reader identify with the narrator and understand her reactions to the journey

    J   teach the reader about the experience of pioneers who settled the western states

The narrative style does not limit the author in doing the things described in choices F, G, and J. The author could do these things with first- or third-person point of view. However, the way to give the reader the closest possible connection to a character is to use that character as the narrator, so choice H is the right answer.

The way in which the narrator expresses herself tells you that she

    A   feels optimistic about the future

    B   is irresponsible with her belongings

    C   puts little effort into doing her chores

    D   thinks about her life in an imaginative way

You know from reading the excerpt carefully that choices A and C are not true. You cannot tell from this excerpt if choice B is true. When you look back at the passage, you can conclude from all of the imagery that the narrator is imaginative, which makes choice D the only possible answer.

© The Continental Press, Inc.   Do not duplicate.

Now read the following excerpt about a young man going to a job interview. Then answer the questions.

A State of Alarm

Oh, why hadn't he set the alarm?

Jake was late.

Where was his suit? He found his interview suit in the back of his closet and threw it on, frantically brushing away the wrinkles. A button was missing. He would have to hide it somehow. Once in his car, he realized with a shock that he had forgotten to check if the car had enough gas to get to the interview. The gas tank was nearly empty. Maybe he could get there. Just barely. He could coast that last hill. He wished he had bought gas yesterday. And why hadn't he looked at his suit?

And the alarm clock! If he'd gotten up only an hour earlier! An hour could have meant a clean suit, no missing button, and enough gas to cross state lines!

When a clerk showed Jake into the manager's office, Jake let go of his jacket for a brief second to shake hands. He sat down quickly, holding his arm awkwardly across the front of his jacket so the manager wouldn't see the gap left by the missing button. Jake answered each question as well as he could, but was a little distracted. He hoped the wrinkles in his suit didn't show as much when he was sitting down.

At the end of the interview, the manager said, "We need people we can count on." He looked at Jake expectantly.

Jake nodded in agreement. "I'm extremely responsible," he said. "Sometimes I think I can be *too* responsible."

"No such thing as too responsible," said the manager. "People sometimes tell me I'm too much of a perfectionist. But I always say that if something is worth doing, it's worth doing well."

Jake nodded again, clutching his jacket even more tightly to his chest.

Unit 1 Responding to a Text

© The Continental Press, Inc.   Do not duplicate.

What is <u>most likely</u> the purpose of the first sentence?

    F to give information about a character's past

    G to explain the theme

    H to describe the characters

    J to hint at the main problem of the story

The first sentence does not give information about a character's past, explain the theme, or describe the characters. Remember that the main problem of the story is that Jake does not allow himself time to prepare for a job interview. If Jake had set the alarm, he could have prevented the problem. Choice J is the right answer.

Jake's <u>main</u> problem in the excerpt is that he is

    A unprepared for a job interview

    B too lazy to put gas in his car

    C unable to find a missing button

    D unqualified for the job he wants

When you look at the excerpt, you can eliminate choices B and C. Although these both may be considered problems in the story, neither is Jake's main problem. There is nothing in the excerpt about Jake being unqualified, so you can eliminate choice D. Choice A is the best answer.

How is Jake's description of himself to the interviewer different from how Jake really is?

    F Jake says that he can be overly responsible, but he is not responsible enough to set his alarm for a job interview.

    G Jake calls himself a very responsible person, but the manager is looking for another answer.

    H Jake acts like he wants the job, but he would rather do another kind of work.

    J Jake is not nervous during the interview, but the manager thinks that he is.

Because you know that Jake was irresponsible about preparing for his interview, you can tell that what Jake says about himself—that he is very responsible—is the opposite of the truth, which makes choice F the only possible answer.

© The Continental Press, Inc.   Do not duplicate.

In the beginning of the story, Jake is upset because he

    A does not notice his jacket was wrinkled and needed a button

    B is unprepared to answer the manager's questions

    C is unsure how to get to the job interview

    D has not given himself enough time to get ready in the morning

> You know that C is not the right choice because Jake was able to get to the interview. He also was able to answer the manager's questions, and he did notice that his suit was wrinkled and missing a button. Choice D is the only possible (and correct) answer.

What is the setting at the end of the story?

    F Jake's home   **H** the gas station

    G Jake's car   **J** an office building

> The story begins at Jake's house and continues in his car on the way to the interview. The end of the story takes place in an office, so J is the best answer.

Which best describes Jake's feelings at the end of the excerpt?

    A relief that he was not too late to the interview

    B fear that the clerk will interrupt the interview

    C hope that the manager does not notice his suit

    D joy that he has been offered the job

> At the end of the excerpt, Jake holds his jacket even more tightly, which shows that he is still concerned with hiding the missing button from the manager. Choice C is the right answer.

The author's purpose in using the third-person point of view is most likely to

    F allow the reader to know all of Jake's thoughts about everything that happens in the story

    G keep the reader's attention focused on what happens in the story

    H allow the reader to understand how the manager feels about the interview

    J give the reader a balanced view of Jake and his unrealistic ideas about himself

> You can tell from the excerpt that Jake would be an unreliable narrator, because the way he describes himself does not match how he really is. The story is written from a limited third-person point of view in order to let the reader see both how Jake sees himself and how Jake really is. Choice J is the correct answer.

© The Continental Press, Inc. Do not duplicate.

Test Yourself

Read the story "At the Fair." Then answer Numbers 1 through 5.

At the Fair
by Leslie Hall

1   Summer had stretched as far as it could go. I don't know exactly when discontent seeped into my heart like water under a door. Nothing new could happen. I got up and went to work at the diner like I always did.

2   I washed dishes in the small room behind the kitchen, where steam billowed out whenever you opened the door. I kept the radio turned up loud and the sound of the churning water in the massive dishwasher would keep time with the music. I spent all summer there, scraping and stacking dirty plates, submerging the heavy white columns in water hot enough to burn, tossing hundreds of plastic cups into the sink, racking up clattering trays of gleaming flatware. I remember the staggered surprise I felt on my first day: how could there possibly be so many plates and bowls in the world? How could there be so many people? How could they possibly eat so much soup, so many sandwiches, so much pie?

3   It was hard work. Over the summer, the muscles of my arms filled out and hardened from the endlessly repetitive lifting and carrying, more demanding than any workout. I didn't miss it when I was away, but I didn't mind it when I was there. I actually liked it. I liked the way the steam came pouring out of the dishwasher when I opened the miniature garage door to let the trays roll out onto the line. I liked the noise, the clanking and clattering, and the careless splashing. I liked how clean I kept the dishroom: the severe clean smell of disinfectant, the shining aluminum sinks as deep as bathtubs. I wore gloves that came up to my elbows and a waterproof apron that almost reached the floor, and I worked furiously, the mad dishwasher of the diner, from the early morning coffee mugs until after the lunch rush of ketchup-smeared plates.

4   "Spoons!" a voice would scream in, and I'd rack them up as fast as I could.

5   Hours could go by; I wouldn't know what time it was, if it were time to eat, how long until I went home. One of the waitresses, Adrienne, a girl who'd just moved here, would usually bring me a plate. She would come in and call my name to let me know that the rush had thinned out, but her voice was so soft I could never hear her over the radio and she would just barely touch my arm to let me know she was there. I'd eat lunch out in the back, sitting on a milk crate, watching the

© The Continental Press, Inc.   Do not duplicate.

street. Nothing ever happened. The delivery truck pulled up at ten, and I helped unload the boxes of lettuce and onions and tomatoes and peaches and strawberries that were going to be chopped and diced and sliced into soups and salads and sandwiches and pies. Around eleven, children marched purposefully down the sidewalk on their way to the city pool. Every day it was hot and sunny and the sky was blue and the sidewalks glared white in the heat. Every day was the same. There was nothing new under the sun.

6   Same songs on the radio that had been playing all summer, same columns of white plates stacking up to forever, same voices yelling for cups, same whoosh of thick steam fogging the room, my own sauna, same picking up hundreds of trays, same putting down hundreds of transparent towers of amber and red plastic cups.

7   School starting in a few weeks. Senior year, nothing new could happen there, either. I had my classes, the same classes all of the other seniors were taking, the same classes my friends were taking. My friends, the same friends I'd had since junior high. Just one more year, a year that seemed like an eternity. I'd play football like I always did, keep my job at the diner, working odd hours when I could, save for college, and the year would go by, just like last year, just like the year before.

8   I wondered if I should get a different job, stop playing football, do something, do anything, anything at all that would shift me off this tedious groove of work-home-school-same-same-same. But I liked my job, liked the rush and torture of football. And school was all right; it was school. I didn't know what could change.

9   When Adrienne brought me lunch, she told me about the fair. We sat behind the diner in the sun and she told me about it. Her voice was bright with pleasure—the roller coaster and the fun house, the lambs and the pigs, the bumper cars! The popcorn! Just listening to her talk about the fair was enough to make you smell the salty popcorn air and see all of the red-striped booths. I hadn't been since I was little, when I still loved the pink sticky clouds of cotton candy, so sweet your teeth ached from looking at it, when I would spend dollars and hours trying to toss dimes into the spinning dishes floating deceptively near. Adrienne said she was going again. It would be the last night. She got up to go back to work.

10   "I'll meet you," I said, before I could think. I said it before I knew what I was saying. Before I could regret it, she gave me a big smile, a smile bright enough to stave off a moment of discontent.

11   I parked in the dirt lot on the side of the hill across the field from the fair and hiked over with a crowd who had done the same: parents with little kids, guys I knew from school, groups of girls. The bright

Unit 1 Responding to a Text

© The Continental Press, Inc.   Do not duplicate.

lights glowed welcome against the inky sky. There was music and laughter and the high-pitched voices of children yelling happily, sticky hands outstretched for more cotton candy, for more dimes to toss, for more lambs to pet, for more tickets to the roller coaster or to the big giant inflatable slide or to the carousel. And she was waiting for me by the ticket booth, with the same beautiful smile I had seen earlier, motioning impatiently at me to hurry so we wouldn't miss a thing.

1 Where does most of the story take place?

   A at the fair   **C** at the diner

   B in a house   **D** in a school

2 Why does the narrator wonder if he should do something different?

   F He feels as if he is stuck in a dull routine.

   G He is afraid his job will interfere with playing football.

   H His friends and family think he works too much.

   J He wants to make a good impression on Adrienne.

3 Read this sentence.

> Before I could regret it, she gave me a big smile, a smile bright enough to stave off a moment of discontent.

   This sentence does all of the following except

   A describe the narrator's pleasant memory about an event from the past

   B foreshadow the ending by showing the change in the narrator's feelings

   C emphasize Adrienne's significance as a character

   D show how Adrienne feels about the narrator

4 The main conflict of the story is between the narrator and

   F Adrienne

   G the tedium of everyday life

   H his family's expectations

   J the children

5 What is most likely the author's purpose in using the first-person point of view?

   A to help the reader understand the narrator's job

   B to create an image of the narrator in the reader's mind

   C to let the reader experience the narrator's emotions

   D to give the reader an objective view of the narrator

© The Continental Press, Inc.   Do not duplicate.

Read the story "The Open Window." Then answer Numbers 6 through 15.

The Open Window
by Saki

"My aunt will be down presently, Mr. Nuttel," said a very self-possessed young lady of fifteen. "In the meantime you must try and put up with me."

Framton Nuttel endeavored to say the correct something which should duly flatter the niece of the moment without unduly discounting the aunt that was to come. Privately he doubted more than ever whether these formal visits on a succession of total strangers would do much towards helping the nerve cure which he was supposed to be undergoing.

"I know how it will be," his sister had said when he was preparing to migrate to this rural retreat; "you will bury yourself down there and not speak to a living soul, and your nerves will be worse than ever from moping. I shall just give you letters of introduction to all the people I know there. Some of them, as far as I can remember, were quite nice."

Framton wondered whether Mrs. Sappleton, the lady to whom he was presenting one of the letters of introduction, came into the nice division.

"Do you know many of the people round here?" asked the niece, when she judged that they had had sufficient silent communion.

"Hardly a soul," said Framton. "My sister was staying here, at the rectory, you know, some four years ago, and she gave me letters of introduction to some of the people here."

He made the last statement in a tone of distinct regret.

"Then you know practically nothing about my aunt?" pursued the self-possessed young lady.

"Only her name and address," admitted the caller. He was wondering whether Mrs. Sappleton was in the married or widowed state. An undefinable something about the room seemed to suggest masculine habitation.

"Her great tragedy happened just three years ago," said the child; "that would be since your sister's time."

"Her tragedy?" asked Framton. Somehow in this restful country spot, tragedies seemed out of place.

"You may wonder why we keep that window wide open on an October afternoon," said the niece, indicating a large French window that opened on to a lawn.

Unit 1 Responding to a Text

© The Continental Press, Inc.   Do not duplicate.

"It is quite warm for the time of the year," said Framton; "but has that window got anything to do with the tragedy?"

"Out through that window, three years ago to a day, her husband and her two young brothers went off for their day's shooting. They never came back. In crossing the moor to their favorite snipe-shooting ground they were all three engulfed in a treacherous piece of bog. It had been that dreadful wet summer, you know, and places that were safe in other years gave way suddenly without warning. Their bodies were never recovered. That was the dreadful part of it." Here the child's voice lost its self-possessed note and became falteringly human.

"Poor aunt always thinks that they will come back some day, they and the little brown spaniel that was lost with them, and walk in at that window just as they used to do. That is why the window is kept open every evening till it is quite dusk. Poor dear aunt, she has often told me how they went out, her husband with his white waterproof coat over his arm, and Ronnie, her youngest brother, singing 'Bertie, why do you bound?' as he always did to tease her, because she said it got on her nerves. Do you know, sometimes on still, quiet evenings like this, I almost get a creepy feeling that they will all walk in through that window—" She broke off with a little shudder.

It was a relief to Framton when the aunt bustled into the room with a whirl of apologies for being late in making her appearance.

"I hope Vera has been amusing you?" she said.

"She has been very interesting," said Framton.

"I hope you don't mind the open window," said Mrs. Sappleton briskly; "my husband and brothers will be home directly from shooting, and they always come in this way. They've been out for snipe in the marshes to-day, so they'll make a fine mess over my poor carpets. So like you men-folk, isn't it?"

She rattled on cheerfully about the shooting and the scarcity of birds, and the prospects for duck in the winter. To Framton it was all purely horrible. He made a desperate but only partially successful effort to turn the talk on to a less ghastly topic; he was conscious that his hostess was giving him only a fragment of her attention, and her eyes were constantly straying past him to the open window and the lawn beyond. It was certainly an unfortunate coincidence that he should have paid his visit on this tragic anniversary.

"The doctors agree in ordering me complete rest, an absence of mental excitement, and avoidance of anything in the nature of violent physical exercise," announced Framton, who labored under the tolerably wide-spread delusion that total strangers and chance acquaintances are hungry for the least detail of one's ailments and

© The Continental Press, Inc.   Do not duplicate.

infirmities, their cause and cure. "On the matter of diet they are not so much in agreement," he continued.

"No?" said Mrs. Sappleton, in a voice which only replaced a yawn at the last moment. Then she suddenly brightened into alert attention— but not to what Framton was saying.

"Here they are at last!" she cried. "Just in time for tea, and don't they look as if they were muddy up to the eyes!"

Framton shivered slightly and turned towards the niece with a look intended to convey sympathetic comprehension. The child was staring out through the open window with dazed horror in her eyes. In a chill shock of nameless fear Framton swung round in his seat and looked in the same direction.

In the deepening twilight three figures were walking across the lawn towards the window; they all carried guns under their arms, and one of them was additionally burdened with a white coat hung over his shoulders. A tired brown spaniel kept close at their heels. Noiselessly they neared the house, and then a hoarse young voice chanted out of the dusk: "I said, Bertie, why do you bound?"

Framton grabbed wildly at his stick and hat; the hall-door, the gravel-drive, and the front gate were dimly-noted stages in his headlong retreat. A cyclist coming along the road had to run into the hedge to avoid an imminent collision.

"Here we are, my dear," said the bearer of the white mackintosh, coming in through the window; "fairly muddy, but most of it's dry. Who was that who bolted out as we came up?"

"A most extraordinary man, a Mr. Nuttel," said Mrs. Sappleton; "could only talk about his illnesses, and dashed off without a word of good-bye or apology when you arrived. One would think he had seen a ghost."

"I expect it was the spaniel," said the niece calmly; "he told me he had a horror of dogs. He was once hunted into a cemetery somewhere on the banks of the Ganges[1] by a pack of pariah dogs, and had to spend the night in a newly dug grave with the creatures snarling and grinning and foaming just above him. Enough to make anyone lose their nerve."

Romance at short notice was her specialty.

---

[1]Ganges: a river in India, which was under the rule of Great Britain when this story was written

Unit 1 Responding to a Text

© The Continental Press, Inc.   Do not duplicate.

6 **Where does the story take place?**

    F at a house in the country   **H** on the banks of a river

    G at a doctor's office   **J** in the rectory of a church

7 **Read this sentence.**

> Privately he doubted more than ever whether these formal visits on a succession of total strangers would do much towards helping the nerve cure which he was supposed to be undergoing.

    What main purpose does this sentence serve?

    A It indicates that Framton is uncertain about his doctor's advice.

    B It hints that Framton's illness may be more serious than he had thought.

    C It suggests that Framton's nerves will be upset later in the story.

    D It shows that Framton is unfamiliar with the people in the country.

8 **Why does Framton go to the country?**

    F to go hunting   **H** his sister told him he should

    G to visit friends   **J** his doctor recommended rest

9 **Which word best describes how the aunt feels while Framton discusses his illness?**

    A bored   **C** cheerful

    B amused   **D** worried

10 **Mrs. Sappleton's niece is best described as**

    F naive

    G serious

    H industrious

    J imaginative

11 **All of the following are clues that this story is set in the early 1900s except**

    A Vera makes a reference to the Ganges, which everyone would have known was a river in India because the country was under British rule until 1947.

    B Framton uses letters of introduction to pay formal social calls, a practice that is no longer common.

    C Framton nearly collides with a bicyclist, but there are no cars in the story.

    D Vera enjoys exaggerating the truth about people when she describes them.

© The Continental Press, Inc.   Do not duplicate.

12 Which word best describes Framton?

    F silly

    G boyish

    H nervous

    J arrogant

13 Why does Framton leave the house so suddenly?

    A Mrs. Sappleton's yawn offends him.

    B He thinks he has seen a ghost.

    C Vera's stories bore him.

    D He is tired and needs to rest.

14 The most likely reason the story is written from the third-person point of view is so the author can

    F give objective descriptions of the characters and insight into their thoughts

    G explain why the niece lives with her relatives

    H provide background information about the cause of Framton's health problems

    J analyze the reason the niece enjoys telling stories

15 BCR Write an explanation that tells why the niece says that Framton is afraid of dogs at the end of the story. Explain how what the niece says relates to the rest of the story. Include details and examples from the story to support your explanation.

Use the lined space to plan your response. Then write your final draft on a separate sheet of paper.

© The Continental Press, Inc.   Do not duplicate.

© The Continental Press, Inc.   Do not duplicate.

Lesson 4

Style and Literary Techniques

An author has many tools to use in order to create different effects for the reader. The author's purpose often influences which tools the author decides to use.

Here are some purposes an author may have for writing:

- to give information
- to persuade the reader to believe or act a certain way
- to entertain the reader
- to give the reader a new way of thinking about a topic
- to help the reader reflect on a concept or an idea
- to create certain feelings in the reader

In this lesson, you will learn about how an author's style and use of literary techniques reveal the author's purpose. Then you will have a chance to practice what you have learned by answering questions about passages you have already read in Lessons 1–3.

1.2.2 The student will determine how the speaker, organization, sentence structure, word choice, tone, rhythm, and imagery reveal an author's purpose.

1.2.3 The student will explain the effectiveness of stylistic elements in a text that communicates an author's purpose.

Style

These indicators refer to the way an author's purpose is communicated through the style of a work of literature. The **style** may be described as the way an author presents the work. Some techniques used to construct the style are:

- the speaker or narrator
- the way the work is organized
- word choice, rhythm, and imagery
- using sentences of different patterns and lengths
- using figurative language and other literary devices

© The Continental Press, Inc.   Do not duplicate.

The style reflects and reveals the author's purpose. It influences how the reader thinks and feels about the writing. When you analyze the style, you examine how the author presents a work of literature and then make a judgment about whether or not the style is effective. Think about these questions as you analyze the style:

- How does the author want me to feel when I read this?

- What techniques does the author use to make me feel this way?

- Do I feel what the author intends? Why or why not?

1.3.3 The student will identify features of language that create tone and voice.

Tone and Voice

Questions measuring this indicator usually ask directly about the tone of the passage or the effect that certain words or phrases have on you as the reader. How does the writing make you feel? Why? The **voice** reveals the attitudes and feelings of the author and contributes to the **tone,** or the overall atmosphere of the writing. Tone and voice are closely connected, and they support the author's purpose. For example, if the author's purpose is to inform, the tone will most likely be straightforward and objective. However, if the author's purpose is to entertain, the tone may be humorous.

The style includes the author's tone and voice, and you can frequently recognize an author's work by a characteristic style. For example, American author Ernest Hemingway is famous for his style, which is characterized by simple declarative sentences, minimal figurative language, and realistic tone.

1.3.1 The student will explain how language and textual devices create meaning.

Diction, Figurative Language, and Literary Devices

This indicator requires you to understand the meaning of special kinds of language and literary techniques that authors use, such as **diction,** or word choice; **figurative language** (including metaphors, similes, and personification); and **literary devices** (including imagery and symbolism).

Literary devices help the author achieve a number of purposes, including the following:

- to make a point in a vivid or memorable way

- to appeal to the reader's senses

© The Continental Press, Inc.   Do not duplicate.

- to make the writing more interesting and fun to read

- to help the reader understand a concept by comparing it to something else

- to create the tone and voice of the writing

- to give the writing identifiable style

Here are some figurative language and literary devices you will need to know:

- *Imagery* includes any figurative language that an author uses to create images in the reader's mind. "The sunlight glittered on the surface of the lake" is an example of imagery.

- *Irony* is the use of words to express something other than (especially, the opposite of) the literal meaning. For example, you are using irony when you say, "Yeah, right" as a reply to something that is the opposite of what you think or feel.

- *Personification* gives human characteristics to things, animals, or ideas. "The highway crept stealthily through the mountains" is an example of personification.

- A *simile* compares one thing to another, using either the word *like* or *as*, such as the sentence "She is growing like a weed."

- A *metaphor* compares two things without using *like* or *as*. The phrase "It's raining buckets" is a metaphor.

1.3.4 The student will explain how devices such as staging, lighting, blocking, special effects, graphics, language, and other techniques unique to a non-print medium are used to create meaning and evoke response.

Elements of Dramatic Literature

Although this indicator refers to non-print medium, on a test you will be asked to answer questions about written plays and dramatic literature. The structure of a play, a story, or a poem helps give the passage meaning. There are literary devices that are used to develop the structure of a literary work. Some of these devices appear only in dramatic literature, such as scene designs; and there are others which may also appear in other works of fiction or poetry, such as dialogue, soliloquies, asides, and character foils.

Here are some functions of different devices:

- *dialogue*—the speech of characters in literature, usually conversation between two or more characters. Dialogue can give insight into the characters' dispositions and their state of mind, give information about the plot, and show conflict between characters.

© The Continental Press, Inc.   Do not duplicate.

- *scene design*—a description of the physical scene in a play, including the setting and props. This is to allow the reader (and, for a play, the audience) to picture the setting intended by the author.

- *aside*—a statement made by a character in a play that is directed to the audience, rather than to another character. Asides may reveal information to the audience about events to come, thus letting the audience know more than the other characters in the play.

- *soliloquy*—a speech by a character who is onstage alone. Usually, a character talks about his thoughts and feelings in a soliloquy.

- *character foil*—a character that provides contrast to another character. For example, a character who cheats and lies can be a foil for a hero who conducts himself honorably.

Guided Practice

Reread page 21, the excerpt from a story about a pioneer family crossing the Rocky Mountains, narrated by a fifteen-year-old girl. Then answer the questions.

Which of the following words best describes the tone of this excerpt?

   A serene

   B ominous

   C lighthearted

   D tragic

> The tone is the overall feeling of the work. As the pioneers get ready to climb the mountains, the author uses images of soldiers and of the pioneers being chased in order to give the reader a feeling of suspense that something bad may be about to happen, which makes choice B the best answer.

What is happening in the third paragraph?

   F The pioneers are worried about crossing the mountains in winter.

   G The pioneers fear the enemy soldiers who are pursuing them.

   H The pioneers tell stories about a snow monster.

   J The pioneers use the sky to predict the weather.

> The first sentence tells you that the pioneers are reaching the mountains. The next sentences describe winter "chasing" the pioneers. Only choice F fits when you go back and look carefully at the third paragraph.

© The Continental Press, Inc.   Do not duplicate.

The effect of the phrase "we could hear the wind whispering" is to help the reader

    A   feel chilled by the wind

    B   think of the wind as a person

    C   hear the sound of the wind

    D   picture the way the wind moves

This question asks you to interpret figurative language. You know that figurative language is language that appeals to the reader's senses. When you realize that the phrase appeals to the sense of hearing, you know that choice C is the best answer.

Read this sentence.

> We could see the clouds gathering snow like soldiers filling ammunition bags.

The phrase "like soldiers filling ammunition bags" lets the reader know that the weather is seen as

    F   a bag

    G   a soldier

    H   an enemy

    J   a landmark

When you look back at the phrase in the context of the passage, you see that the weather is creating an obstacle for the pioneers. This helps you know that the purpose of the phrase is to show the reader that the weather is an enemy to the pioneers. Choice H is the best answer.

Read this sentence from the excerpt.

> The clean fragrance of the soap and the sunshine and the sounds of the birds all seemed like a dream to me now...

The purpose of this sentence is to give the reader

    A   details about the setting

    B   clues about future events

    C   a description of the character

    D   information about past events

This sentence from the excerpt is a flashback. You know that a flashback is the literary device an author uses to look back at events from the past. Only choice D tells why an author would use a flashback.

Unit 1 Responding to a Text

© The Continental Press, Inc. Do not duplicate.

Reread the excerpt from page 24 about a young man going to a job interview. Then answer the questions.

What is ironic about how Jake describes himself to the interviewer?

F   Jake says that he can be overly responsible, but he is not responsible enough to set his alarm for a job interview.

G   Jake calls himself a very responsible person, but the manager is looking for another answer.

H   Jake acts like he wants the job, but he would rather do another kind of work.

J   Jake is not nervous during the interview, but the manager thinks that he is.

Because you know that Jake was irresponsible about preparing for his interview, you can tell that what Jake says about himself—that he is very responsible—is the opposite of the truth, which makes choice F the only possible answer.

Read these sentences from the excerpt.

And the alarm clock! If he'd gotten up only an hour earlier! An hour could have meant a clean suit, no missing button, and enough gas to cross state lines!

The most likely purpose for these sentences is to

A   give the reader insight into Jake's conflicts about getting a job

B   let the reader know Jake's thoughts

C   warn the reader to allow adequate time to prepare for job interviews

D   let the reader know more about the setting

The sentences are a narrative version of Jake's thoughts as he is rushing to the interview. This makes choice B the only possible answer.

© The Continental Press, Inc.   Do not duplicate.

Reread the poems by Emily Dickinson and Onitsura on page 16. Then answer the questions.

In the first stanza of her poem, Dickinson implies that the "traveling flake of snow"

    F cannot make a decision

    G must run away from home

    H has lost something important

    J cannot agree with anyone

Look back at the poem for clues about the meaning of this phrase. In line 4, the word "debates" is a clue that personification is being used to portray the snowflake as indecisive. Choice F is the best answer.

In Onitsura's poem, the "pine-tree voices" most likely refer to

    A people talking from behind the trees

    B people whispering nearby

    C the sound of the wind in the trees

    D the poet's inner thoughts

Because the haiku is so brief, it may be helpful to look at the answer choices to see which are not present in the poem. There are no people, so you can eliminate A and B. The poet does not refer to himself at all, so choice D is also likely to be incorrect. However, the poet is describing a scene in nature, and choice C, the sound of the wind in the trees, makes the most sense.

Which phrase is used to show a comparison between people and objects?

    F the clouds are mean

    G across a barn

    H through a rut

    J cool are the breezes

When you review the answer choices, you can eliminate G and H because they do not have any words that would make you think about either object as a person. You can also eliminate J, because the temperature does not indicate that the breezes are like people. Only choice F makes a comparison between the clouds and people.

Unit 1 Responding to a Text

© The Continental Press, Inc.   Do not duplicate.

Test Yourself

Reread the story "At the Fair" on pages 27–29. Then answer Numbers 1 through 7.

1 Look back at Paragraph 1 of the story. What is ironic about the sentence, "Nothing new could happen"?

   A The narrator will soon begin a new school year.

   B The narrator has just begun working at a new job.

   C The narrator's feelings change when he goes to the fair.

   D The narrator's friends convince him to stay on the football team.

2 The main purpose of the questions at the end of Paragraph 2 is to make the reader feel

   F the energy of the cooks

   G the hunger of the customers

   H the weariness that the waitresses must feel

   J the shock and surprise the main character feels

3 The phrase "discontent seeped into my heart like water under a door" means that the narrator became unhappy in a way that was

   A confusing

   B unexpected

   C sudden and quick

   D slow and gradual

4 Which of these phrases from the story is used to show the narrator's boredom with his life?

   F the churning water in the massive dishwasher would keep time with the music

   G boxes of lettuce and onions and tomatoes and peaches and strawberries

   H a smile bright enough to stave off a moment of discontent

   J this tedious groove of work-home-school-same-same-same

5 How does Adrienne's character serve as a foil to the narrator in Paragraph 9?

   A Her kindness in bringing him lunch contrasts with his self-centeredness.

   B Her quiet voice contrasts with his enjoyment of loud music.

   C Her enjoyment of the fair contrasts with his feelings of unhappiness.

   D Her sociable nature contrasts with his solitary temperament.

© The Continental Press, Inc.   Do not duplicate.

6 Read this sentence.

> There was music and laughter and the high-pitched voices of children yelling happily, sticky hands outstretched for more cotton candy, for more dimes to toss, for more lambs to pet, for more tickets to the roller coaster or to the big giant inflatable slide or to the carousel.

All of the following describe how this sentence is typical of the author's style except that it

F   uses words that rhyme

G   uses descriptive language

H   repeats words or phrases

J   is a long, complex sentence

7 BCR Write an explanation that tells how the author's use of language creates the tone of the story. Include details and examples from the story to support your explanation.

Use the lined space to plan your response. Then write your final draft on a separate sheet of paper.

Unit 1 Responding to a Text

© The Continental Press, Inc.   Do not duplicate.

_____

_____

_____

_____

_____

_____

_____

_____

_____

_____

Reread the story "The Open Window" on pages 30–32. Then answer Numbers 8 through 11.

8 **What is ironic about Framton's predicament at the end of the story?**

    F He tells complete strangers about his health problems.

    G He fails to understand why some people like to hunt.

    H He is under doctor's orders to remain quiet and calm.

    J He finds it difficult to converse with the two women.

9 **Which of these words best describes the tone of the story?**

    A reflective

    B suspenseful

    C inspirational

    D gloomy

10 **Which of these pairs of words best describes the author's voice?**

    F gleeful and joking

    G amused and ironic

    H nervous and worried

    J bewildered and uncertain

11 **What does the last line of the story mean?**

    A Vera enjoys reading novels with heroes and heroines.

    B Vera finds the story of her aunt and uncle romantic.

    C Vera is known for telling untrue but imaginative stories.

    D Vera has fallen in love with Framton.

Unit 1 Responding to a Text   **45**

© The Continental Press, Inc.   Do not duplicate.

Read "Sammy Sosa Comes Home." Then answer Numbers 12 through 16.

Sammy Sosa Comes Home
by Ruben Gonzalez

1   He seemed a giant

Stepping forth from the plane that Tuesday morning,

Even without his war club,

His weapon, emblazoned with the number 66.

5   We were all giants that day

As he touched his heart to us,

And told us how happy he was to be ours.

He shared his glory with us at the airport,

And along the highway from the capital,

10   And through the dusty streets of San Pedro de Macorís,

That mother of *beisbol* players,

Where shortstops spring up between the rows of sugarcane,

And pitchers learn their craft with balls of rags.

He came home to us,

15   One who had been pursued in the land of the *Yanquis*

(And paraded in the city of the Yankees).

And the people in the cardboard *barrios,*

Forgetting for one day the *huracán* that left them homeless,

Became for one hour Sammy Sosa,

20   Watching the *pelota* rise out of Wrigley Field in the afternoon sun,

As high and distant as any dream.

12 The phrase "We were all giants that day" intends to show that the speaker feels that Sammy Sosa
F   was proud of the people in his town
G   was from a family of very tall people
H   grew up in a town where people were taller than the usual height
J   made the people of his hometown feel proud of him and of themselves

13 What is the "weapon" in line 4?
A   a war club
B   a baseball bat
C   a catcher's mitt
D   a ball of rags

Unit 1 Responding to a Text

© The Continental Press, Inc.   Do not duplicate.

14 In lines 17 and 18 of the poem, the poet suggests that people's pride in Sosa's achievements allowed them to

    F temporarily escape from their troubles

    G think of a new way to solve their problems

    H dream their own dreams of a bright future

    J hope to become baseball players one day

15 Which of these pairs of words <u>best</u> describes the tone of the poem?

    A proud and triumphant

    B cheerful and amused

    C nostalgic and hopeful

    D sympathetic and affectionate

16 The author's purpose in writing this poem was <u>most likely</u> to

    F describe what it is like to play professional baseball

    G explain how to become a professional baseball player

    H give information about the place where Sammy Sosa grew up

    J show how Sammy Sosa's success affected the people of his country

© The Continental Press, Inc.   Do not duplicate.

Lesson 5

Responding to and Interpreting Text

When you read, you respond to or interact with the text. Often, you have some kind of personal response or feeling about what you have read. You may feel moved by the language or feel sympathy for the characters as you interpret their feelings. Perhaps you have a deep understanding of a theme as it relates to your life. You may make a judgment about the literary merit or the quality of the writing. These are only some of the responses you might have to literature, your interpretation of the meaning, and the way it affects you.

Instead of **Guided Practice,** in this lesson you will see some examples of brief constructed-response (BCR) or extended constructed-response (ECR) questions that require a literary response and interpretation. On a test, of course, your response to these questions would be in writing. Under your teacher's direction, you may want to try writing an essay to answer these sample questions, or discuss how you would answer them. You will have an opportunity to write two essays in the **Test Yourself** section. In Unit 2, you will learn more about writing essays and other compositions.

1.3.2 The student will interpret a work by using a critical approach (e.g., reader response, historical, cultural, biographical, structural) that is supported with textual references.

1.3.6 The student will assess the literary merit of a text.

Literary Interpretation and Criticism

These indicators require you to assess or interpret literature from a critical point of view, using various approaches. These approaches include reader response, historical, cultural, and biographical.

Some test questions ask you to describe or explain your response, giving supporting evidence from the passage. Supporting evidence may include specific details or words and phrases from the passage that support your response or point of view.

Reader Response Approach

Looking at literature from the reader's, or from your own point of view is one way to analyze literature. In this approach, you as the reader actively respond to and interpret the writing.

© The Continental Press, Inc.   Do not duplicate.

Here is an example of a brief constructed-response (BCR) question that asks for a personal (reader) response:

> **Reread the poems "The Sky Is Low, the Clouds Are Mean" and "haiku" on page 16. Write an explanation that tells your feelings in response to reading these poems. Include specific details and examples from the poems to support your explanation.**

Here is an example of a writing task (ECR) that asks you to take a reader response approach to literary criticism:

> **Reread the poem "Sammy Sosa Comes Home" on page 46.**
>
> **The poem "Sammy Sosa Comes Home" reveals the speaker's hero worship of the baseball player Sammy Sosa. What qualities do you feel are necessary for a hero? Do you feel that Sammy Sosa, as described in the poem, has those qualities?**
>
> **Write a well-organized essay about the qualities you feel are necessary for a hero. Explain whether or not you feel that Sammy Sosa, as he is described in the poem, has those qualities. Support your ideas with appropriate details and examples from the poem.**

Here is another example of a writing task (ECR) that asks for a personal response:

> **Reread the story "At the Fair" on pages 27–29. In the beginning of the story, the narrator feels as if he is stuck in a routine. By the end of the story, his feelings have changed to feelings of hope and anticipation. What happened to change the narrator's feelings? Does this change seem genuine?**
>
> **Write a well-organized essay about how the narrator's feelings changed in the story. Include your own ideas about the change in his feelings, how the change occurred, and whether or not the change is genuine. Support your ideas with appropriate details and examples from the story, your own personal experiences, or from both.**

Historical and Cultural Approaches

Learning about the period or place in which literature is written will help you have a deeper, more meaningful understanding of the work. Just as the author's background is reflected in literature, so is the time period and the culture in which the work was written. The major historical events, cultural and social issues, and political and economic concerns are often interwoven in a work of literature. John Steinbeck's *In Dubious Battle* describes the rise of the labor movement and unions when the United States was battered by the Great Depression. In the same time period, Ralph Ellison's *The Invisible Man* and Richard Wright's *Native Son* have themes that are intertwined with the stigma and horrible consequences of racism. Many of Dawn Powell's novels, such as *The Magic Island* and *Angels on Toast,* criticize the overly ambitious, self-centered,

© The Continental Press, Inc.   Do not duplicate.

superficial approach to life Powell observed in New York City in the 1920s and 1930s.

Here is an example of a writing task (ECR) that asks you to take a cultural and historical approach to literary criticism:

> **Reread the poems "The Sky Is Low, the Clouds Are Mean" and "haiku" on page 16.**
>
> **Emily Dickinson and Onitsura wrote their poems in different time periods. They were from different countries that have different cultures.**
>
> **Write a well-organized essay about the influence that these differences in culture and time period may have had on the poems. Support your ideas with appropriate details and examples from both poems.**

Biographical Approach

Knowing about an author can enrich your understanding of literature. The author's background, attitudes, and feelings usually are reflected in the author's work. For example, the Hispanic author Sandra Cisneros draws upon her cultural heritage and background in her novel *The House on Mango Street*. In a similar way, turn-of-the-century American author Edith Wharton draws from her background in writing *The Age of Innocence*, a novel that reflects Wharton's upper-class social standing and New York upbringing.

As with personal responses, writing tasks that ask you to take a certain approach in criticizing literature will require that you use supporting evidence from the reading passage to support your interpretation. Your evidence may include specific words, phrases, details, or examples from the passage.

Here is an example of a writing task (ECR) that asks you to take a biographical approach to literary criticism:

> **Reread the story "The Open Window" on pages 30–32.**
>
> **The writer Hector Hugh Munro, also known as "Saki," was born in Burma and raised in England. He later traveled all over the world.**
>
> **Write a well-organized essay about the influence that these experiences in Hector Hugh Munro's life may have had on his writing. Support your ideas with appropriate details and examples from the story.**

© The Continental Press, Inc.   Do not duplicate.

Test Yourself

Chief Joseph (1840–1904) was a Nez Percé Chief who was best known for his resistance to the U.S. government's attempts to force his people onto a reservation. Read the following excerpt from a speech that he gave when he visited Washington, D.C., in 1879. Then do the writing task that follows.

…Good words do not last long unless they amount to something. Words do not pay for my dead people. They do not pay for my country.…They do not protect my father's grave. They do not pay for all my horses and cattle. Good words will not give me back my children. Good words will not make good the promise of your war chief.…Good words will not give my people good health and stop them from dying. Good words will not get my people a home where they can live in peace and take care of themselves.

I am tired of talk that comes to nothing. It makes my heart sick when I remember all the good words and all the broken promises. There has been too much talking by men who had no right to talk. Too many misrepresentations have been made, too many misunderstandings have come up between the white men about the Indians.

If the white man wants to live in peace with the Indian, he can live in peace. There need be no trouble. Treat all men alike. Give them the same law. Give them an even chance to live and grow. All men were made by the same Great Spirit Chief. They are all brothers. The earth is the mother of all people, and all people should have equal rights upon it.

You might as well expect the rivers to run backward as that any man who was born a free man should be contented when penned up and denied liberty to go where he pleases. If you tie a horse to a stake, do you expect he will grow fat? If you pen an Indian up on a small spot of earth and compel him to stay there, he will not be contented, nor will he grow and prosper. I have asked some of the great white

© The Continental Press, Inc.   Do not duplicate.

chiefs where they get their authority to say to the Indian that he shall stay in one place while he sees white men going where they please. They cannot tell me.

…When I think of our condition, my heart is heavy. I see men of my race treated as outlaws and driven from country to country or shot down like animals.

I know that my race must change. We cannot hold our own with white men as we are. We ask only an even chance to live as other men live. We ask to be recognized as men. We ask that the same law shall work alike on all men. If the Indian breaks the law, punish him by the law. If the white man breaks the law, punish him also.

Let me be a free man—free to travel, free to stop, free to work, free to trade where I choose, free to choose my own teachers, free to follow the religion of my fathers, free to think and talk and act for myself—and I will obey every law or submit to the penalty.

Whenever white men treat Indians as they treat each other, then we will have no more wars. We shall all be alike—brothers of one father and one mother, with one sky above us and one country around us, and one government for all. Then the Great Spirit Chief who rules above will smile upon this land and send rain to wash out the bloody spots made by brothers' hands from the face of the earth.

ECR

> Chief Joseph spoke eloquently about the injustices that were done to his people. Write a well-organized essay in which you discuss how listeners who first heard his speech must have felt, and what made them feel that way. Support your ideas with appropriate details and examples from the speech.

Use page 53 to plan your essay. Then write your essay on a separate sheet of paper.

© The Continental Press, Inc.   Do not duplicate.

© The Continental Press, Inc.   Do not duplicate.

Now read "Song of the Freedmen" and the background information. Then do the writing task that follows.

Song of the Freedmen

We are coming from the cotton fields,
We are coming from afar;
We have left the plow, the hoe, the axe,
And we are going to war.
We have left the old plantation seat,
The sugar and the cane,
Where we worked and toiled with weary feet,
In sun and wind and rain.

Refrain 1:
Then come along my boys,
O, come, come along,
Then come along my brothers,
O come, come along.

We are coming from the cotton fields,
We are coming from afar;
We have left the plow, the hoe, the axe,
And we are going to war.
We will leave our chains behind us, boys,
The prison and the rack;
And we'll hide beneath a soldier's coat
The scars upon our back;
And we'll teach the world a lesson soon,
If taken by the hand,
How night shall come before 'tis noon,
Upon old Pharaoh's land.

Unit 1 Responding to a Text

© The Continental Press, Inc.   Do not duplicate.

BACKGROUND INFORMATION

No one knows who wrote "Song of the Freedmen." It appeared in 1864 and spread quickly through the ranks of African American soldiers in the Civil War. This was two years after Congress had authorized the enlistment of "persons of African descent" into the Union Army.

African American soldiers fought in every theater of war, from Virginia to Texas. Their most famous exploit was the assault on Fort Wagner, South Carolina, by troops of the 54th Massachusetts regiment on July 18, 1863. The attack failed, and more than 40 percent of the all-black regiment were killed. But they were a heroic example to other African Americans—and to white Northerners who had doubted the wisdom of arming them. "The arm of the slaves [is] the best defense against the arm of the slaveholder," said former slave Frederick Douglass. "Who would be free themselves must strike the blow." Altogether, some 185,000 African Americans put on Union blue. Some were free blacks from the Northern states, but most were former slaves who had fled to Union lines for the chance to fight. "Song of the Freedmen" was their song.

ECR

Write a well-organized essay in which you discuss how the theme of "Song of the Freedmen" is related to the social issues of the time period in which it was written. Support your ideas with appropriate details and examples from the song and the background information, your own knowledge, or both.

Use page 56 to plan your essay. Then write your essay on a separate sheet of paper.

© The Continental Press, Inc.   Do not duplicate.

© The Continental Press, Inc.   Do not duplicate.

WRITING COMPOSITIONS

The goal of the lessons in Unit 2 is to give you guidance in writing different kinds of compositions, including essays with specific forms and language that is appropriate for a particular audience and purpose.

You need to do two kinds of writing on the Maryland HSA English test: brief constructed responses (BCR) and extended constructed responses (ECR). In this unit, you will learn how to write essays (ECR), but the same techniques apply for both kinds of writing tasks.

Lesson 1

Writing Strategies

Whether you are writing a letter, an essay, a book report, or a story, the process for writing is usually the same: You get ideas about what you want to say, make notes, draft some writing, and then revise, proofread, and correct your work in order to produce a final draft.

> **2.2** The student will compose texts using the prewriting, drafting, revising, and editing strategies of effective writers and speakers.

The stages of your writing should look something like this:

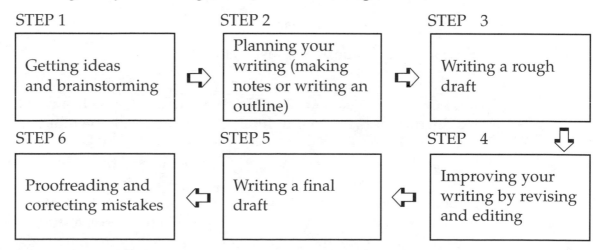

STEP 1
Getting ideas and brainstorming

STEP 2
Planning your writing (making notes or writing an outline)

STEP 3
Writing a rough draft

STEP 6
Proofreading and correcting mistakes

STEP 5
Writing a final draft

STEP 4
Improving your writing by revising and editing

© The Continental Press, Inc.   Do not duplicate.

On a test, you would be asked to write one of these compositions. You have probably written many of them for school assignments.

- A *biographical narrative* is writing about another person. It may be a famous person, an historical figure, or someone in your life. An *autobiographical narrative*, of course, is about you.

- A *short story* is a short piece of fictional writing that is usually about a specific event or a character's experience, and has a clear beginning, middle, and end.

- A *personal essay* is an essay written to express your own thoughts, ideas, feelings, or beliefs.

- A *response to literature* is an essay about something that you have read.

- An *informational essay* is an essay in which you explain something.

- In a *persuasive essay, letter,* or *speech,* you are writing to convince someone to think as you do or to take a certain action.

2.2.1 The student will use a variety of prewriting strategies to generate and develop ideas.

Prewriting

This indicator focuses on the time you spend reading a test question and thinking about what to write in your essay. Make sure you understand the writing task before you begin. Even if your writing is good, your score could be affected if your writing does not meet all of the requirements of the task.

Read the writing task carefully to make sure you understand:

- the topic for your writing

- who is your intended audience or reader (this could be a teacher, other students, people in your community, etc.)

- your purpose for writing

- what your composition must include

Whatever the type of writing, it's always a good idea to spend some time thinking about what you are going to write before you begin. When you are looking for ideas for your writing, always start with the topic. Ask yourself questions about the topic. Consider what you already know. Sometimes it helps to brainstorm your ideas. Writing quickly and without correcting yourself, list every idea you have about a certain topic—even if one of the ideas seems silly or does not seem to fit. For example, suppose the assignment is to write a personal essay about important qualities of a friend. One student's brainstorm list might look something like the one at the top of the next page.

© The Continental Press, Inc.   Do not duplicate.

```
┌─────────────────────────────────────────────┐
│            Qualities of a Friend              │
│   1. kindness                                 │
│   2. generosity                               │
│   3. fun to be with                           │
│   4. going to the Boardwalk                   │
│   5. jokes                                    │
│   6. good times                               │
│   7. Carlos—good listener                     │
│   8. Jan—always helpful and encouraging       │
└─────────────────────────────────────────────┘
```

This student wrote a list of words and phrases about what friendship means to her. She crossed out one item on her list because it does not fit in with the other words and phrases. After reviewing her list, this student might write an essay about her friends Carlos and Jan, and how these two friends demonstrate the qualities of friendship in the way they are willing to listen and be helpful.

Once you have decided what you are going to write about, you can jot down your ideas, notes, or an outline on scratch paper to organize your ideas before you begin writing. A good outline is especially useful when you have a limited amount of time to write or if you do not have time to write a first rough draft.

Drafting If you have time, you may want to write a rough draft on scratch paper first and then copy a final draft into the booklet provided. Writing a separate rough draft lets you make revisions without having to cross out whole sentences or even paragraphs. If you feel you don't have time to write a separate rough draft, organize your ideas as much as possible before you begin writing.

Here are some important things to consider about your writing:

- Your writing should be well-organized, interesting to read, and appropriate for your intended purpose and reader. One simple way to organize your composition is to make sure it has an introduction, a body, and a conclusion. If you are writing a story, make sure it has a clear beginning, middle, and end.

- Using sentences of different lengths and patterns will help keep your reader interested. Readers may get bored by an essay that only has short sentences or sentences that always begin the same way.

- In choosing the words and style for your composition, think about your purpose and reader. You would probably use a casual, friendly style of writing in a letter to a friend and a more formal style when writing an assignment for a teacher.

- Always be sure to include specific details and examples to support your main idea and to make your writing interesting to the reader.

Remember that your writing will be read and scored by a real person, so write clearly and neatly. If you need to make corrections, use one line to strike through your mistake and then write your correction above it. Be sure to make your writing as easy to read as possible.

© The Continental Press, Inc.   Do not duplicate.

Lesson 2

Audience and Purpose

Every time you write, you have a purpose. Your purpose for writing may be to express your thoughts and ideas, or to describe a person, event, or place that is memorable. You may be writing in order to tell somebody something or to explain how to do something. A school assignment might ask you to analyze or evaluate literature that you have read.

Your purpose for writing will influence what you say and how you say it, even if the topic is the same or very similar. For example, if you are writing a letter to the manufacturer of a portable music player in order to request a refund because the product you bought was defective, you will write differently than if you are writing an e-mail to your friend in which you complain about the poor sound quality of your new portable music player.

In much the same way, your audience has an influence on your writing. Your audience is your reader. If you write a letter requesting permission to stage a social event at school, your audience is most likely the principal, the school board, or another authority figure. If you write a letter to the editor suggesting solutions for a community problem, your audience is the people in your community who read the newspaper. Because you want your writing to accomplish your purpose, you need to choose language and a style that will have the greatest effect on your audience.

> **2.2.2** The student will select and organize ideas for specific audiences and purposes.

The focus of this indicator is on your ability to understand the purpose and audience for which you are writing and to choose your words and ideas accordingly. For example, when you write to your friends, casual language is in order. That is the style of language you use with your friends every day. Your friends might feel distant if you use formal, academic language. However, if you are writing a business letter, a friendly, casual style would be inappropriate and would not be taken seriously.

© The Continental Press, Inc.   Do not duplicate.

Guided Practice

Answer the questions that follow.

Read this sentence:

> Using the services of ZipTravel.com in preparing for our journey enhanced the quality of our travels.

Revise this sentence for a <u>younger audience</u>.

- **A** Our vacation was more fun because we used ZipTravel.com to plan our trip.
- **B** We especially enjoyed our travels because the level of service provided by ZipTravel.com was superb.
- **C** ZipTravel.com offered the best value for our money.
- **D** Best as it is

If you are revising for a younger audience, you want to use simple, relatively informal language. Choice A is the best answer.

Read this sentence:

> Even though they look like something out of a sci-fi movie, the rows of windmills make you think of the past.

Revise to a more <u>formal</u> style.

- **F** The windmills look modern with all that metal, but they still have a kind of old-fashioned style.
- **G** Despite its rather futuristic appearance, the windmill orchard calls to mind the quaint and picturesque.
- **H** Even though the windmills are very shiny and gleaming and sleek, they still look as if they're from long ago.
- **J** Best as it is

When revising to achieve a more formal tone, you want to avoid casual language, such as "kind of," and contractions, such as "they're." Choice G is the correct answer.

© The Continental Press, Inc.   Do not duplicate.

Read this sentence:

> As far as I'm concerned, the principal's crazy new rule about not going off campus is stupid.

Revise this sentence so it is <u>less likely to offend the audience</u>.

    A It's my personal belief that the closed-campus policy is unfair to students.

    B I think the principal's decision to close the campus makes no sense.

    C My opinion is that closing the campus is mean and hurts students.

    D Best as it is

To revise the sentence so it is less offensive, you want to avoid using words like "mean," and you will try to find a more diplomatic way of making your point than to say the policy "makes no sense." Choice A is the best answer.

Read this sentence:

> Harnessing energy from the wind can be positive in significant ways, but it can also be inconvenient and troublesome.

Revise for an <u>audience of your peers</u>.

    F Wind power is good in some ways and bad in others.

    G The utilization of wind from turbines as a means of securing power has its benefits; it is also accompanied by some difficulties.

    H As with any power source, there are advantages and disadvantages to using wind turbines.

    J Best as it is

To revise the sentence to be appropriate for your peers, you need to use language that is clear and easy to understand. Choice F is too simple, but choice G is too complex and formal. Choice H is the answer that fits best.

Unit 2 Writing Compositions

© The Continental Press, Inc.   Do not duplicate.

Test Yourself

Answer Numbers 1 through 5.

1 **Read this sentence from a note to a neighbor:**

> It's probably no surprise to you that the sound of those rusty hinges and the banging of that old gate drive me out of my mind, so do something about it.

Revise this sentence so it is <u>less likely to offend</u> the neighbor.

A You may not realize that the sounds of the gate closing can be heard loudly inside our house; we would appreciate it if you would repair the gate so it closes quietly.

B You must hear the horrible, screeching sounds that you make every time you open or close that broken-down gate, so we want you to fix it.

C Maybe you like the way your gate is so loud that it wakes up the whole neighborhood, but we don't; either fix it or tear it down.

D Best as it is

2 **Read this sentence from an employee handbook:**

> You've got to let your boss know if you are running late or you have to get off work early.

Revise this sentence to a <u>more appropriate style</u> for the workplace.

F If you are going to be late, or if you need to leave early, it is your responsibility to notify your supervisor.

G The person in charge has to be told if you can't get in on time or you've got to leave early.

H When you find you must deviate from your regular schedule in any way, whether you must arrive after the commencement of the work day or whether you must depart earlier, it is your obligation to inform the person to whom you report.

J Best as it is

Unit 2 Writing Compositions

© The Continental Press, Inc.   Do not duplicate.

3 Read this sentence from an announcement to publicize a school event:

> There will be some kind of a spring celebration on Friday with lots of good things to do and there will be food, too.

Revise this sentence so it is <u>more likely to interest the audience</u> in attending the celebration at the school.

  A The Spring Fair will be held on Friday and will be nice for everyone; also, bring your appetite because there will be lots of food.

  B Friday's Spring Fling is sure to be a winner, with fun games, crazy contests, terrific prizes, and great food. Don't miss it!

  C Come to the Spring Party, which will have interesting events and a great deal of food to eat.

  D Best as it is

4 Read this sentence from a speech:

> Everybody should do some kind of volunteer work because it feels good to help people, and people need help, and it helps the place we live, too.

Revise this sentence to a <u>formal</u> style.

  F When people help other people, they are actually helping themselves and others in the community, too.

  G If you volunteer, it makes lots of people feel better: you, the person you work with, and everyone around you.

  H Volunteering is beneficial to the volunteer, the recipient of the assistance, and the community as a whole.

  J Best as it is

5 Read this sentence from a letter to the editor:

> Gas prices keep going up, and we need to take care of the matter soon.

Revise this sentence so it is <u>more likely to influence the audience</u>.

  A High gas prices could possibly be inconvenient, so let's try to do something.

  B The increase of the price of gas might make life hard for someone, so we need to think about it.

  C Skyrocketing gas prices will soon be a serious problem unless we take immediate action.

  D Best as it is

Unit 2 Writing Compositions

© The Continental Press, Inc.   Do not duplicate.

Lesson 3

Writing to Inform

When you write to inform, your purpose is to communicate information to your reader. You may explain a process, describe how to do something, explain a cause and effect, or inform the reader about an event or a situation. In the workplace, you might write a memo or business letter to communicate information.

Because your purpose is to provide information, your writing needs to be as clear and easy to understand as possible. Unlike writing for self-expression, informational writing does not include the writer's thoughts, feelings, and beliefs about the topic. This writing is usually straightforward and objective. You won't use as much figurative language as you might in a story, a poem, or other types of prose.

2.1.1 The student will compose to inform by using appropriate types of prose.

This indicator focuses on choosing appropriate language for informational writing.

Select your tone and language carefully. Both should be appropriate for the task and the audience. If you are writing an e-mail to give a friend directions to your house, your tone and language will probably be casual and friendly and even humorous. However, if you are writing a research report or an informational essay for your teacher, your tone and language will probably be a little more formal.

While it is always necessary to plan your writing, planning takes on even more importance when you are writing to inform. Here are some steps to follow:

1. **Identify your topic.** You may be writing to complete an assignment or for a specific purpose, in which case your topic may already be clear to you. If you are writing for a test or school assignment, make sure you understand all of the requirements of the writing task.

2. **Gather your information.** If you are writing a research paper or report, you will probably need to go to the library to do some research. Take careful notes so that you have all the information you need when you begin writing. Don't forget to document your sources. If you are writing for a test, you won't be doing research beforehand. But taking notes as you read a passage on a test is an important step.

Unit 2 Writing Compositions   **65**

© The Continental Press, Inc.   Do not duplicate.

3. **Organize your notes and information.** How are you going to approach your topic? You might organize your notes in time order if you are writing a history report or in the order of steps in a process if you are writing about how to do something.

4. **Plan your writing.** Make an outline or some other kind of organizational structure that will help you organize the ideas in your writing. Make sure you are using a logical sequence so readers will understand your writing.

5. **Start writing!** A rough draft is always a good idea. Unless you are writing for a test, ask someone else to read your writing. Ask the person if there is anything that is difficult to understand or that does not make sense. This will help you revise your writing. For information on how to revise your writing, go to Lesson 7 of this unit.

Guided Practice

Read this task that asks you to write to inform others. Use a separate sheet of paper to plan your essay. Then write your essay on another sheet of paper.

ECR

Think about something you know how to do. It can be a simple task, such as sewing a button onto a shirt, changing a flat tire on a bicycle, or changing the oil in a car. There might be a sport that you play well, such as football or soccer. What does a person need to know and be able to do in order to do this? What are the steps involved?

Write an essay in which you explain how to do something that you know how to do. Include details about the activity, the steps involved, and the materials or equipment needed. Make sure your essay is fully developed and logically organized.

For this essay, you would first decide what task you are going to explain. Suppose you want to explain how to sew a button on a shirt. You would think about what materials you need, then make a list, such as: sewing needle, thread, a button, the shirt. Next, you would think about the steps of the process and write them on your draft. This would include: finding a button and/or thread that matches the color of your shirt, threading the needle, and sewing the button to the shirt. After organizing your ideas and deciding how to explain each step, you would begin writing your essay.

© The Continental Press, Inc.   Do not duplicate.

Test Yourself

Read the writing task. Use the space below to plan your essay. Then write your letter/essay on a separate sheet of paper.

ECR

Suppose that tenth-grade students in another country have contacted students at your school because they are considering coming to your school as exchange students, and they want to know what your school is like.

Write a letter to one of these foreign students to inform this student about what it is like to be a high school student at your school. You may describe a typical day at your school and write about your classes, sports, clubs, or social life at school. Include details and examples in your writing. Make sure your letter is fully developed and logically organized.

© The Continental Press, Inc.   Do not duplicate.

Lesson 4

Writing to Persuade

When you write in the persuasive mode, you are trying to convince the reader to believe as you do or to take a specific action. Persuasive writing is common in everyday life. Newspaper ads and television and radio commercials are written to persuade people to buy products and services. Letters to the editors of magazines and newspapers are generally persuasive letters. Legislators receive persuasive letters from constituents who want them to vote in certain ways or to pass or repeal laws.

You have probably already written persuasive letters, speeches, or essays. You may have written a note to your parents to persuade them to let you attend a special event or stay out later than your curfew. You would write a letter to try to persuade a potential employer to interview you for a job. If you debate, you give persuasive speeches. You have probably written persuasive essays as school assignments.

2.1.4 The student will compose persuasive texts that support, modify, or refute a position and include effective rhetorical strategies.

This indicator requires you to write persuasively in response to various situations. For a test, you might be asked to write a persuasive letter, speech, or essay. No matter what form your persuasive writing takes, you will need to choose a position on an issue or topic, and then construct a solid case for your position.

Your persuasive writing will need to contain:

- a clear statement of your position

- logical reasons why you think the way you do

- specific, detailed examples to support your position

- persuasive language and effective communication (rhetorical strategies)

You may also use persuasive techniques to influence or appeal to your reader.

© The Continental Press, Inc.   Do not duplicate.

Common Persuasive Techniques

Bandwagon—influencing people by implying that "everyone" supports one's position or candidate. The bandwagon approach is all about peer pressure. The idea is that "everyone" is doing something, so you should do it, too.

Card-stacking—offering only one side of an issue to support one's position.

Elitism—linking a candidate, concept, or product with high social standing, education, wealth, or fame.

Glittering generalities—using glittering generalities is to focus on the positive qualities without referring to any negative qualities.

Name-calling—also known as mud-slinging, which means to point out negative qualities of the opposing position or candidate while ignoring any positive qualities.

Plain folk—appealing to the common point of view, or using language that signals that the candidate or other product users are not elite, but are just like everyone else.

Repetition—saying the same message or using the same words or phrases more than once in order to make an impression on the reader or listener.

Testimonial—using endorsements from celebrities or other people.

Transfer—using a symbol to carry a message. An automobile manufacturer might use a symbol of an eagle as part of its logo in order to seem both strong and all-American.

Here are some questions that will help you plan and organize your persuasive writing:

• What is my position on this issue?

• What do I want the reader to think or believe?

• What action do I want the reader to take?

• How can I get the reader to do what I want or to believe as I do?

• Which reasons and examples will best support my position?

• Which words and phrases will be most effective in persuading the reader?

© The Continental Press, Inc.   Do not duplicate.

Guided Practice

Read this persuasive writing task. Use a separate sheet of paper to plan your essay. Then write your essay on another sheet of paper.

ECR

Suppose your county has a problem with overcrowding in the elementary schools, but some of the high schools, including the one you attend, are not filled to capacity. The local school board has decided to close one high school and turn it into an elementary school in. Your school is under consideration for closure.

Write a letter to the local school board in which you support *or* oppose the closure of your high school. Include a clear statement of your position and specific details and examples to support your position. Be sure to use persuasive language.

For this task, you would first take a position on the issue. Let's say that you think the school board should leave your school open and find another solution to the overcrowding problem in the elementary schools. Now, think of logical reasons that you might take this position. One reason might be that your school is an important part of your community's history. Another might be that students at your school have consistently high academic performance, while students at another high school might not. Think of specific supporting examples. After organizing your ideas, you would begin writing.

Test Yourself

Read the writing task. Use the next page to plan your essay. Then write your essay on a separate sheet of paper.

ECR

The famous football coach Knute Rockne said, "Life is competition." People compete in sports, in the workplace, economically, and even socially. Is competition helpful or harmful? In what ways may competition be helpful or harmful?

Write a persuasive essay in which you take a position indicating whether competition is helpful or harmful. Include a clear statement of your position and specific details and examples to support your position. Be sure to use persuasive language.

Unit 2 Writing Compositions

© The Continental Press, Inc.   Do not duplicate.

© The Continental Press, Inc.   Do not duplicate.

Lesson 5

Writing for Self-Expression

Writing for self-expression means writing in order to express your own ideas, thoughts, feelings, and beliefs. This is highly personal writing that is often reflective or creative. Writing for self-expression may include writing in a journal or web log ("blog"); writing letters or e-mails to family and friends; writing essays on topics that matter to you; writing a memoir, a diary, or other autobiographical writing; and writing stories, poems, or even songs.

Because you are writing to express your own ideas, there is no wrong way to approach this mode of writing. However, if you want others to read and understand your writing, or if you are writing to complete a school assignment or a section of a test, you will want to follow basic guidelines about writing. These include organizing your ideas, using clear language that the reader will understand, supporting your ideas with details or examples, and choosing words carefully in order to add interest to your writing.

2.1.2 The student will compose to describe, using prose and/or poetic forms.

2.1.3 The student will compose to express personal ideas, using prose and/or poetic forms.

These indicators focus on writing for self-expression. Because self-expressive writing is an opportunity to be creative, you may want to use figurative language and other literary devices in order to create vivid images and appeal to the reader's senses. Sometimes you write descriptions as part of self-expressive writing, such as when you describe the setting of a story. The use of literary devices can be especially effective in descriptive writing.

A writing task on a test may ask you to write one of the following:

- an autobiographical or biographical essay (writing that is about yourself or another person)

- a personal narrative (a story about yourself)

- a short story (short fictional writing)

- a personal essay (an essay in which you write about your own ideas, thoughts, feelings, or beliefs)

© The Continental Press, Inc.   Do not duplicate.

Guided Practice

Read this biographical writing task. Use a separate sheet of paper to plan your essay. Then write your essay on another sheet of paper.

ECR

Jackie Robinson overcame prejudice and racial discrimination in order to play major league baseball. What traits do you believe are necessary to overcome challenges and become successful?

Write an essay in which you describe someone who has succeeded by overcoming challenges. What personal traits did this person need in order to succeed? How did these traits help this person overcome challenges to become successful? Include specific examples and details to support your writing.

For this task, you would first think of a successful person who has overcome obstacles. Let's say that you decide to write about Helen Keller. Now, think of the personal traits she needed in order to overcome her challenges of impaired sight and hearing. How did these traits help her achieve an education and go on to become a famous writer and lecturer? What examples can you use from Helen Keller's life to support your main idea? Think of specific supporting examples and details. After organizing your ideas, you would begin writing.

Test Yourself

Read the writing task. Use the next page to plan your essay. Then write your essay on a separate sheet of paper.

ECR

Think of a goal you have or a dream you would like to achieve. What would you have to do to make your goal or dream a reality?

Write an essay as if you have already met your goal or reached your dream. Describe what it is like to have done what you wanted to do. Explain what it feels like to see your dream come true. Include specific details and vivid language in order to make your writing more interesting.

© The Continental Press, Inc. Do not duplicate.

© The Continental Press, Inc.   Do not duplicate.

Lesson 6

Research

2.3.1 The student will identify sources of information on a self-selected and/or given topic and assess their appropriateness to accomplish a purpose.

Identify Sources of Information

This indicator and other indicators in this lesson focus on doing research. On a test, you may be asked to answer questions about what sources to use and where to find information about a given topic. When you research a topic for a project or term paper, you need to find the best sources for the information you need. For example, if you are writing a report about efforts to save an endangered species of butterflies in the Brazilian rain forest, you might need information about the region's current butterfly population. The best source of up-to-date information may be the Web site for an organization dedicated to the preservation of endangered species, a current issue of the magazine *National Geographic*, the Web site operated by the Smithsonian Institution, a recent article from the newspaper, or an encyclopedia that has been recently updated.

On the other hand, if you are writing a research paper about President John F. Kennedy, you would want to use books that contain biographical information about President Kennedy. The date of publication would be less important because it is unlikely that much of the historical information about President Kennedy has changed recently.

Choosing a reference source depends not only on your topic, but on your purpose. Some sources, although limited, may have just the information you need. For example, if you had already gathered sufficient biographical information about President Kennedy, but still needed to find out the date he first took office, you could easily find that information in a biographical dictionary. However, a biographical dictionary will not contain enough information to be the primary source of information for your research paper.

When looking at different sources of information for research, here are some questions to ask:

- What are the best sources for different kinds of information?

- What are the limitations of each source?

- Which sources are likely to have the most current information?

- What features of the sources will help me find the information I need?

© The Continental Press, Inc.   Do not duplicate.

2.3.2

The student will use various information retrieval sources (traditional and electronic) to obtain information on a self-selected and/or given topic. Electronic sources include automated catalogs, CD-ROM products, and online services like Internet, World Wide Web, and others.

Once you have identified good sources, you need to be able to use the features of the sources to find specific information related to your research topic. Titles, chapter titles, tables of contents, lists of illustrations, indexes, appendices, glossaries, and footnotes are all features that will help you find information in printed text sources, such as books and magazines. You can also use features such as headings, subheadings, illustrations, captions, call-out boxes, sidebar text, and bold or italic print to locate and understand the information you need; these features appear in printed text and online text. Online text may also have features such as pull-down menus, Web site directories, and links to additional information or related topics. You may also need to use an online library catalog or an Internet search engine. In both cases, you would need to use key words or phrases, an author's name, or the specific title of a reference source in order to find the source you need.

Guided Practice

Now answer these questions.

Which of these would be the <u>most</u> effective method to learn more about student travel discounts?

  A make an appointment to interview the travel agent at each travel agency that offers student discounts

  B ask other students for information about their favorite travel destinations

  C skim the newspaper for travel-related articles and advertisements for airlines and other transportation agencies

  D review the Web sites of different airlines and travel agencies for information about student travel discounts

When you skim all the possible answers, you can see that only choices A and D refer to student travel discounts. Remember that you are not only interested in student travel discounts, but you need to choose the *most effective* method of learning about student travel discounts. Choice A is likely to take much more time and energy than choice D, so choice D is the right answer.

© The Continental Press, Inc.   Do not duplicate.

Chris is using a book about rocks and minerals as a source for her research paper about how crystals form. Which of these features would Chris use to find the definition of an unfamiliar word from the book?

F   the index
G   the glossary
H   the table of contents
J   the list of illustrations

To answer this question, you need to know the terminology of book features and how to use them to find the information you need. You know that the table of contents tells the titles of the chapters in the book and that the list of illustrations tells only about the illustrations. The index at the back of the book lists topics and ideas covered in the book and page numbers so the reader can find specific information easily and quickly. Only the glossary gives definitions for specific words or phrases. Choice G is the answer that fits.

Which key words will be most effective to find information about how carbon transforms into diamonds?

A   valuable gems
B   diamond cutting
C   diamond mining
D   diamond formation

Two of the choices that refer specifically to diamonds, B and C, do not relate to how diamonds form. Choice A is too broad to be helpful in a key word search, as there are many kinds of valuable gems. Choice D, diamond formation, is the best answer.

Which of these would be the best source of information about Aaron Burr's legendary encounter with Alexander Hamilton?

F   "Accusation of Treason," an article published on the Family Education Network Web site
G   "The Aaron Burr Trial," an article published on the University of Missouri-Kansas City Law School Web site
H   *The Intimate Life of Alexander Hamilton*
J   *The Duel: Alexander Hamilton, Aaron Burr, and the Future of America*

You can eliminate choices F and G because an article is less likely to have as much information as a book. In addition, the titles of both articles give clues that the articles are too narrowly focused to provide comprehensive information on the duel between the two men. The book listed in choice H focuses primarily on Alexander Hamilton. This means that choice J, which is the only reference with a title that focuses on the specific research topic, is correct.

Unit 2 Writing Compositions

© The Continental Press, Inc.   Do not duplicate.

2.3.3 The student will use a systematic process for recording and documenting information.

Record, Organize, and Document Information

After locating the information for your research paper, the next steps are to:

1. use a system for taking notes and organizing information

2. document your sources

One way to take notes and organize information is to use a web like this:

In the center of the web, you would write the main idea of what you are reading or the topic of your research. Then you would write supporting details in the outer circles.

Another way to record and organize information is to use a graphic organizer. Look at this paragraph about early skateboards. Then look at the graphic organizer that follows. The graphic organizer shows the main idea and supporting details.

> The first skateboards were actually like homemade scooters. They were made almost a hundred years ago, in the early 1900s. Kids would remove the wheels from their roller skates and fasten them onto boards. They would mount a wooden crate on the front of the board. Handles attached to the crate made the scooters (or skateboards) easier to control and steer.

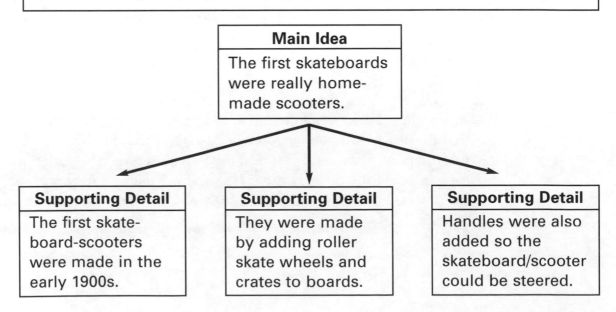

Unit 2 Writing Compositions

© The Continental Press, Inc.   Do not duplicate.

Once you have done your research and organized the information you have gathered, you will begin writing your research paper. You need to make sure that you have documented all of your sources so that you can cite the information sources in your writing.

It is important to document the title, author(s) or editor(s), publisher, date and location of publication, and the page number(s) of the pages that contain the information. Many students find it helpful to use 3×5 cards to document sources. Here is an example:

Title: Diamonds: Nature's Jewelry

Author(s): Leo Elze

Page numbers: 25–35 (crystal formation); 51 (hardness of diamonds); 75–78 (diamond mining)

Date Published: 2002

Publisher: GeoMatters, Inc.

Location: Chicago

When you document your sources in the bibliography of your research paper, the bibliographic entry for this book would look like this:

Elze, Leo. Diamonds: Nature's Jewelry. Chicago: GeoMatters, Inc., 2002.

The author's or editor's name appears first, followed by the title, location of publisher, publisher's name, and date of publication.

Guided Practice

Read this paragraph and answer the two questions that follow.

When Bruce Cook made a presentation to a school in Mercer Island, Washington, students had the opportunity to see something unusual: a boat being built. A Native American artist from Alaska, Bruce Cook is a Haida. The Mercer Island boat was actually a replica, a smaller version of a traditional native canoe, carved from a single cedar log. Students watched as Cook shaped the wood with a steel adz and a wooden mallet. As he worked, Cook lectured about Native American culture. Students participated by keeping journals for English classes about the progress Cook made on the canoe. Students also wrote research papers about some aspect of Native American life or culture. Cook and his canoe even infiltrated math class, when students took measurements of the canoe.

© The Continental Press, Inc.   Do not duplicate.

In his research paper, Terry wants to write about the idea that the ancient art of boat building may be endangered in the Native American community. Which fact should be included in his notes?

  A Bruce Cook's model was three feet long.

  B Bruce Cook is an artist who was raised in Alaska.

  C Students learned about the cedar tree in science class.

  D Few people know how to build canoes in the traditional way.

When you read all of the possible answers, you can see that choice D is the only possible correct answer. The clue is the word "endangered," which tells you that boat building is practiced by fewer people today than in the past.

If Terry's focus is the art of boat building, which fact is <u>least</u> important to include in his notes?

  F the location of Mercer Island

  G the names of tools used to shape the wood

  H how a traditional canoe looks when it is finished

  J how Native Americans teach their children to make canoes

After reading the answer choices, you can see that choice F is the correct answer. The clue is that choice F is the only answer that does not give information that is specifically related to canoes or boat building.

Unit 2 Writing Compositions

© The Continental Press, Inc.   Do not duplicate.

Use the paragraph and graphic organizer to practice taking notes and organizing information.

A few daring riders took the crates off their boards. But true skateboards were not invented until the 1950s, when surfing was riding a wave of popularity in California. Some inventive surfers found a way to sidewalk surf by putting wheels on a board. Surfboard manufacturers saw an opportunity and began to manufacture and sell skateboards in 1963. However, these vintage skateboards did not give the smooth ride or allow for the tricks that skateboarders perform today because the wheels on these vintage skateboards were made of clay and did not grip the road well.

Here is what the graphic organizer might look like after you fill in the information:

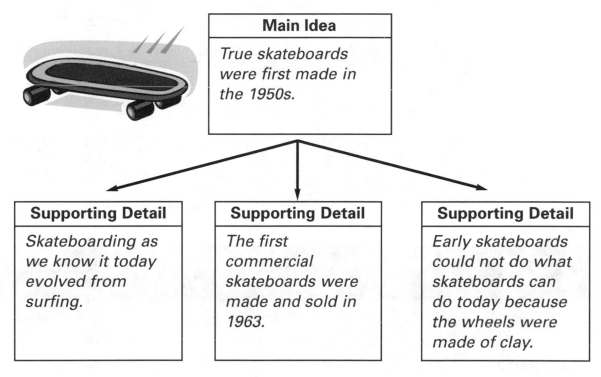

Main Idea

True skateboards were first made in the 1950s.

Supporting Detail

Skateboarding as we know it today evolved from surfing.

Supporting Detail

The first commercial skateboards were made and sold in 1963.

Supporting Detail

Early skateboards could not do what skateboards can do today because the wheels were made of clay.

Unit 2 Writing Compositions

81

© The Continental Press, Inc.   Do not duplicate.

Use the information below to answer the question.

> **Title:** Human Mind, Machine Mind: A Study of Intelligence
>
> **Author(s):** Vin Rai
>
> **Page numbers:** 55–75 (history of artificial intelligence)
>
> **Date Published:** 2002
>
> **Publisher:** Herald Books
>
> **Location:** New York

Which is the best way to write a bibliographic entry for this book?

    A Rai, Vin. Human Mind, Machine Mind: A Study of Intelligence. New York: Herald Books, 2002.

    B Vin Rai, Human Mind, Machine Mind: A Study of Intelligence. Herald Books: New York, 2002.

    C Human Mind, Machine Mind: A Study of Intelligence. Vin Rai. New York: 2002, Herald Books.

    D Human Mind, Machine Mind: A Study of Intelligence. New York: Herald Books, 2002. Rai, Vin.

In a bibliographic entry, the author's name always appears first. This eliminates choices C and D. The location of the publisher comes before the publisher's name. Choice A is the best answer.

2.3.5 The student will synthesize information from two or more sources to fulfill a self-selected or given purpose.

Synthesize Information

Once you have completed your research and organized your information, you will need to synthesize, or put together, pieces of information from different sources in order to discuss your topic or prove a point. When you perform research, you might use as many as 10 or 15 reference sources. Then you have to put that information together in a way that makes sense to you. How does the information in one source support the information in another source?

If you were writing a research paper on the civil rights movement, you might learn from one source that President Lyndon B. Johnson was deeply committed to defeating segregation and promoting civil rights. In another source, you might learn that President Johnson appointed the African American lawyer and civil rights activist Thurgood Marshall to the Supreme Court. One way to synthesize this information is to say that the appointment of Thurgood Marshall to the Supreme Court is evidence of President Johnson's commitment to civil

© The Continental Press, Inc.   Do not duplicate.

rights, because he was willing to face opposition to appoint the best man for the job, and because he wanted to appoint someone who would continue to fight for civil rights as a Supreme Court justice.

Guided Practice

Now read "Nutrition Made Simple," the nutrition label, and sample menu. Then answer the questions.

Nutrition Made Simple

Nutrition is chemistry, but that doesn't mean it is difficult to understand. Think of your body as an engine; the food you eat is the fuel. Just as your car won't run if you forget to put in gasoline, your body will fail to function at an optimal level unless you eat food that meets your body's nutritional requirements.

Nutrition Labels and How to Read Them

In order to educate consumers about the nutritional values of their food purchases, food manufacturers are required to label foods with detailed information about their nutritional content. In addition to listing the food's ingredients, the nutrition label also lists the number of calories the food contains as well as the amounts, if any, of protein, fat, carbohydrates, vitamins, minerals, and dietary fiber. By reading labels carefully, you can determine which foods are better choices in terms of their nutritional value and make informed choices in order to eat a healthful diet.

Calories

Look first at the number of calories and the serving size. Compare the serving size listed on the label to the amount of food you

Here is a sample nutrition label from a cereal box:

Nutrition Facts	
Serving size: 3/4 cup (1.5 oz)	
Servings per container: About 13	
Amount per serving	
Calories 190	**Calories from Fat 25**
	% Daily Value**
Total Fat 3 g*	5%
Saturated Fat 0 g	0%
Cholesterol 0 mg	0%
Sodium 95 mg	4%
Potassium 300 mg	9%
Total Carbohydrate 36 mg	12%
Dietary Fiber 8 g	32%
Sugars 13 g	
Protein 9 g	14%
Vitamin A 0%	Vitamin C 0%
Calcium 5%	Iron 7%
Phosphorus 9%	Magnesium 9%
Copper 7%	

*Amount in cereal only

**Percent Daily Values based on a 2,000 calorie diet. Depending on your daily calorie needs, your daily values may be higher or lower.

Calories per gram:
Fat: 9   Carbohydrate: 4   Protein: 4

Ingredients: Whole rolled oats, rye, barley, brown rice, buckwheat, sesame seeds, wheat, evaporated skim milk, textured soy protein, evaporated sugar cane juice concentrate, maple syrup, oat flour, rice flour, whole wheat flour, wheat bran, rice bran, oat bran, sunflower oil, honey, salt, vanilla, cinnamon, dried apricots.

Unit 2 Writing Compositions

© The Continental Press, Inc.   Do not duplicate.

normally consume in one sitting. You may notice that your own personal serving is two or three times the actual serving size determined by the manufacturer. If you are counting calories, this information will be useful.

Calories are the units of energy that your body burns as fuel. If you burn more calories than you eat, you lose weight. If you burn fewer calories than you eat, you gain weight. Exercise is one way to burn excess calories and help keep your calorie output in balance with your calorie intake. How many calories do you need? The average man may need 2,300 calories per day, depending on his level of activity. The average woman needs slightly fewer calories: about 2,000 per day.

List of Ingredients

Next, scan the list of ingredients, which are listed in the order of the amount contained in the food, from the largest amount to the smallest. This may be surprising. Sugar makes a frequent appearance in the list of ingredients, often appearing as the leading item on the list. It's actually not so surprising when you consider that sugar is appealing to the taste buds. However, because sugar does not contain any nutrients that your body needs, it is an ingredient that your body finds completely unnecessary at best. For people who are diabetic or who have a genetic tendency to become diabetic, sugar may even be harmful.

Daily Values

Next, review the vitamins and minerals carefully. The amounts of these nutrients are listed as percentages of the amount your body needs on a daily basis, or the "daily values." Some foods and drinks, such as cereal, bread, and even orange juice, may be fortified with extra vitamins or minerals.

Carbohydrates, Proteins, and Fats

Finally, examine the label to find the amounts of carbohydrates, proteins, and fats in the food. These are the building blocks of food:

- carbohydrates are starches, easily converted into energy readily used by the body

- proteins contain the chemicals required to build muscles, organs, and bones

- fats are a very concentrated form of energy

A gram of fat has nine calories of food energy, compared to the four calories in a gram of carbohydrates. Fat is such a concentrated form of energy because it actually stores energy. When you eat more calories than you need for energy, whether the calories come from fat, carbohydrates, or protein, the extra fuel converts to fat and is stored by your body for future use.

© The Continental Press, Inc.   Do not duplicate.

Don't let the idea of eating fat frighten you; everyone needs a certain amount of fat in order to maintain good health. There are some chemicals found only in fats that your body requires in order to function properly. But many people do eat far more fat than they need, just as people tend to eat too much sugar, simply because fats, like sugar, improve the taste of food.

Dietary Guidelines

What constitutes a healthy diet? The United States Department of Agriculture regularly suggests guidelines for a healthy diet. In 2005, the USDA created Dietary Guidelines. The Dietary Guidelines describe a healthy diet as one that:

- emphasizes fruits, vegetables, whole grains, and fat-free or low-fat milk and milk products

- includes lean meats, poultry, fish, beans, eggs, and nuts

- is low in saturated fats, *trans* fats, cholesterol, salt (sodium), and added sugars

Here's a sample menu for one day that fulfils most people's daily needs according to the Dietary Guidelines:

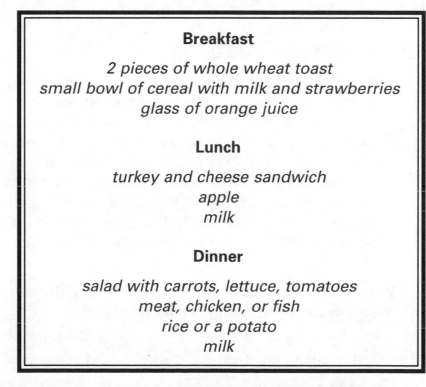

Breakfast

2 pieces of whole wheat toast
small bowl of cereal with milk and strawberries
glass of orange juice

Lunch

turkey and cheese sandwich
apple
milk

Dinner

salad with carrots, lettuce, tomatoes
meat, chicken, or fish
rice or a potato
milk

Once you've met your nutritional requirements, a treat would be a harmless indulgence that you might consider. Remember, occasional servings of sweets or extra fats are not harmful when consumed in moderation. Just make sure treats don't replace nutritious foods entirely.

© The Continental Press, Inc.   Do not duplicate.

Now Put It All Together

Let's say you need 2,000 calories per day. You go to a fast-food restaurant for lunch and have a cheeseburger (510 calories, half of which come from fat), a medium order of French fries (340 calories, half of which come from fat), and a medium soda (108 calories, no fat, but contains no nutritionally valuable substances). Total: 958 calories. The bad news is that although you've consumed about half your daily calorie allowance, you might even still be hungry.

Looking on the bright side, you've eaten a third of your daily protein requirement and 25 percent of the vitamin C you need. But there's definitely room for improvement; the down side is that you could have met more of your nutritional requirements had you eaten healthier foods.

A Change Is in Order
You can make better food choices without launching a boycott of fast-food restaurants. Substitute a grilled or broiled chicken breast sandwich (290 calories, about one-fifth from fat) for the cheeseburger, and replace the fries with a salad and low-fat dressing (170 calories). Choose milk (110 calories, but with a much higher nutritional value) instead of soda. This order change adds up to 570 calories, rather than 958, and meets many more of your daily nutritional needs.

Small Changes Add Up

You don't have to decide today that you are going to follow the Dietary Guidelines to the letter and eat only healthy, sugar-free, fat-free foods from now on. Be realistic. You will want to go out to lunch with your friends, so you need to figure out how to make good food choices most of the time, in different places, and under varying circumstances. Some days you'll want a treat, such as buttered popcorn at the movies or ice cream after dinner. But little changes, such as eating a salad at lunch or drinking milk or juice instead of soda, can add up to good nutrition and a more healthy way of life. It's as simple as that.

Which of these foods would be the <u>least</u> healthy substitute for the glass of orange juice in the sample menu on page 85?

    A a glass of milk   **C** some blueberries

    B half a grapefruit   **D** a cup of hot chocolate

Looking at both the menu and the article will help you answer the question. The article states it is best to avoid adding extra sugar to the diet. The only answer that contains added sugar is choice D, which is the best answer.

© The Continental Press, Inc.   Do not duplicate.

Which of these would be the healthiest substitute for the lunch in the sample menu?

    F   a cheeseburger, French fries, and a glass of water

    G   a hot dog with chili and cheese and a milk shake

    H   a salad with chicken and cheese, a wheat roll, and fruit juice

    J   carrot and celery sticks with dip, orange juice, and potato chips

When you review the information in the article with the lunch items on the sample menu, you can see that the lunch menu includes meat, grain, milk, and fruit. The only answer choice that includes all these kinds of food and excludes less healthy food selections is choice H.

According to the article, which ingredients in the nutrition label should be eaten sparingly, if at all?

    A   sugar cane juice and sunflower oil

    B   whole rolled oats and sesame seeds

    C   textured soy protein and wheat bran

    D   brown rice and evaporated skim milk

Look at the nutrition label on page 83 and the information in the article. You read in the article that fats and sugars are to be eaten sparingly. When you look at the nutrition label and the answer choices, you can see that the only possible answer is choice A because, unlike the other answer choices, it gives ingredients that contain both fat and sugar.

Which group of food is <u>not</u> represented by any of the ingredients in the nutrition label?

    F   fruits

    G   vegetables

    H   fats and sugars

    J   milk and milk products

Look at the Dietary Guidelines on page 85. Then review the nutrition label on page 83. The only food group in the answer choices that is not represented in the ingredients list is vegetables. Choice G is the best answer.

© The Continental Press, Inc.   Do not duplicate.

Test Yourself

Answer Numbers 1 through 4.

1 Which of these would be the best source of information about scandals surrounding the International Olympic Committee in the late 1990s?

    A   a reprint of the speech by the International Olympic Committee president at the opening ceremony of the 2002 Olympic Games at http://multimedia.olympic.org/pdf/en_report_286.pdf

    B   a compilation of radio news programs, "Olympic Bribery Scandal," including a timeline and an overview, on the National Public Radio Web site at http://www.npr.org/programs/specials/ioc/

    C   *Olympic Athletes*, published 2003

    D   *The Olympics at 100: A Celebration in Pictures*, published 1995

2 Maya found a snake in her backyard. Which of these would be the most effective research method to identify the species of the snake?

    F   check a glossary of biological terms

    G   look in the encyclopedia under the heading "snake"

    H   review the illustrated reptile field guides on eNature.com

    J   call the local pet store to see if the store has similar snakes for sale

3 Which of the following would be the best source of information about caring for a pet snake?

    A   a Web site run by a snake owner

    B   a call-in radio show hosted by a local veterinarian

    C   *Snakes as Pets*, published in 2001

    D   "Snakes: In the Home or In the Wild?" an article in a nature magazine

4 Which feature of a magazine would be most helpful to a reader who is trying to find a specific article?

    F   the illustrations

    G   the advertisements

    H   the table of contents

    J   the copyright page

© The Continental Press, Inc.   Do not duplicate.

Read "Good Health! Good Job!" Then answer Numbers 5 through 7.

Good Health! Good Job!

Here's a riddle: You are in a room that is very clean. In the room you see a computer and some medical equipment. A woman wearing a white coat is taking care of you. What is her occupation?

If you guessed a doctor, you could be right. But, she could also be a nurse, a technician, a **pharmacist,** or an **optometrist.** There are many different jobs in health care. There are opportunities to work in hospitals, clinics, nursing homes, doctors' offices, drugstores, laboratories, and with emergency care. Volunteering at a hospital is one way to learn about all the different jobs in a hospital. As a volunteer, you may have the opportunity to assist with patient care, support services, and administration.

The Patient's Friends

Hospitals employ hundreds of people, but only some of them are doctors and nurses. Not everyone on the nursing staff is a nurse. Nurse's aides and nursing assistants do many jobs to help the nurses. They help move patients from one place to another, keep the hospital clean, and see that there are supplies in place. Sometimes volunteers help with these jobs.

Hospital **dieticians** plan and make patients' meals. They have to know what foods are good for people who are sick or are getting better. They can help people plan ways to eat to stay healthy. And hospitals have offices where staff members handle records and other business.

There are **technicians** who help patients with special tests. Technicians operate the machines that do x-rays and scans to show what is inside the body. It's their job to see that the test is clear so the doctors can read the information.

There are also laboratory technicians. After a doctor or nurse takes a sample, such as blood, from a patient, the lab technician does tests on the sample. This technician gives the doctor test results; with this information the doctor can often tell what is wrong.

pharmacist (FARM-uh-sist): *n. a person who studies medicines and fills prescriptions for medicine*

My cousin is a *pharmacist* at a local drugstore.

optometrist (op-TOM-uh-trist): *n. a person who examines your eyesight*

The *optometrist* recommended that I get glasses.

dietician (die-eh-TISH-un): *n. a person who specializes in what people should eat to be healthy*

The *dietician* planned meals for Granddad that were low in fat.

technician (tek-NISH-un): *n. a person who is skilled in a special field or process*

The dental *technician* took x-rays of my teeth.

Unit 2 Writing Compositions

89

© The Continental Press, Inc.   Do not duplicate.

5 This excerpt includes call-out boxes in the margins. The text in the boxes helps the reader by

    A explaining the work of a dietician

    B listing different healthcare professions

    C describing the people who work in a hospital

    D giving definitions of words that might be unfamiliar

6 Which feature helps the reader predict the topic of the excerpt?

    F the title

    G the bold print

    H the first sentence

    J the paragraph indents

7 What is an optometrist?

    A a nurse

    B a technician

    C a person who administers vision tests

    D a person who makes dietary recommendations

Use the information below to answer Numbers 8 through 10.

Title: The Spirit of Flight

Author(s): Arlene O. Jackson

Date Published: 2005

Publisher: Winfield University Press

Location: Minneapolis, Minnesota

---

8 In a bibliographic entry, which information would appear <u>first</u>?

    F Jackson, Arlene O.   **H** The Spirit of Flight

    G Minneapolis, MN   **J** Winfield University Press

9 In order to quote from the author of this book in a research paper, a reader would also need to document

    A definitions from the glossary

    B topics included in the index

    C the number of chapters listed in the table of contents

    D the page numbers on which the quotation originally appeared

Unit 2 Writing Compositions

© The Continental Press, Inc.   Do not duplicate.

10 Chanda is writing a report in which she discusses several early inventions which contributed to the eventual success of human flight. Which of these is the <u>best</u> way for her to organize the information she has gathered in her research?

   F record only the main ideas from each reference source

   G record the author's name, book title, and publisher information

   H copy down most of the information she reads so she will have the most information possible

   J take notes in a chart with columns so she can easily compare similarities and differences among the inventions

Read "The Great Mars Math Mistake" and "The Red Planet." Then answer Numbers 11 through 13.

The Great Mars Math Mistake

In 1998, NASA—the National Aeronautics and Space Administration—launched two missions to Mars. They were timed to take advantage of the planet's closest approach to Earth, which takes place every 26 months. One of the two spacecrafts was called the Mars Climate Orbiter. Its name described its job exactly. It was meant to fly in an orbit around Mars, gathering data on the planet's climate. Scientists hoped to keep track of how Mars' temperature changes over time. They wanted to find out about dust, water vapor, and gases in Mars' atmosphere. Eventually, the Climate Orbiter would help communicate with future bases on Mars.

The spacecraft was supposed to reach its Mars orbit on September 23, 1999. It never did. It came in at too low an altitude. And so it was caught by the planet's gravity and crashed into the surface.

What Went Wrong?

NASA investigators began looking into what went wrong at once. It seemed that there had been signs of trouble months before the spacecraft reached Mars. Computers usually plot a course through space with pinpoint accuracy. The Climate Orbiter kept drifting away from where the computers said it should be. Because the differences were so slight, the scientists figured the computers were wrong.

But they weren't. It turned out that the problem lay with the Climate Orbiter's thrusters. These tiny jets were part of a system

© The Continental Press, Inc.   Do not duplicate.

designed to keep the craft on course. In space, there's a constant flow of radiation in all directions from the sun. This "solar wind" tended to roll the spacecraft over. The thrusters were supposed to help correct its position. But in fact, they were pushing the spacecraft off course. The push was tiny—but it was big enough to wreck the Climate Orbiter.

Measurement Mix-Up

It was the reason the thrusters had failed that outraged NASA. The company that built them had measured their thrust in *pounds.* That's a unit from the English system of measurement. NASA's computers figured thrust in *newtons*—a unit from the metric system.

That was the huge mistake. Science always uses metric units. NASA had asked for metric units. But NASA's engineers had dropped the ball, too. They had failed to correct for the difference between the two systems. One pound of force equals about 4.45 newtons. The difference is very small. But it meant a death sentence for the Mars Climate Orbiter.

A pound measures force as well as weight. It's the force needed to make a one-pound object move one foot per second faster every second.

Everyone Makes Mistakes

NASA had been sleeping on the job in other ways too, its own investigators said. It hadn't assigned enough people to the project. The engineers had not been trained adequately in how the spacecraft worked. There had been poor communication between different groups. A key course-correction step hadn't been made.

Oh yes—that second mission to Mars launched around the same time as the Climate Orbiter? It was called the Mars Polar Lander. It was supposed to study the Martian soil and look for signs of life. It landed on Mars on December 3, 1999, but it was never heard from again.

The Red Planet

Perhaps because Mars is Earth's neighboring planet, it has long been a subject of fascination for Earthlings. As early as July of 1965, the United States sent a probe, *Mariner 4,* to take photographs of the surface of Mars, revealing no evidence of water or life on this planet. More than 30 years later, *Pathfinder* reached Mars after traveling through space for seven months.

Of all the planets in our solar system, Mars is the only planet scientists believe may have supported some form of life at one time. It is unlikely that life on Mars was similar to life on Earth, since the atmospheres of the two planets are so different. The atmosphere on Mars contains primarily carbon dioxide with some nitrogen.

© The Continental Press, Inc.   Do not duplicate.

Although there does not appear to be evidence of any life on Mars now, there are indications that some kind of life may have existed on Mars in the past. Scientists believe they have detected what may be fossils of basic life forms in meteors from Mars.

Historical U.S. Expeditions to Mars

Mariner 4 finds no evidence of water or life on Mars.	1965
Mariner 9 orbits Mars and takes satellite photographs of volcanoes on Mars.	1971
Viking 1 lands on Mars. Sends weather news to the U.S. every day until 1983.	1976
Pathfinder lands on Mars.	1997

11 Which is <u>most likely</u> the reason the Climate Orbiter is excluded from the timeline?

   A There is little published information about the Climate Orbiter.

   B The Climate Orbiter was unsuccessful in achieving its mission.

   C The mission of the Climate Orbiter was the same as the mission of the Pathfinder.

   D The Climate Orbiter was launched the same year as the Viking 1.

12 Look back at the passage about the Climate Orbiter and the excerpt about Mars on pages 94–96. According to the information in the passages, which statement is probably true?

   F Human life will be found on Mars.

   G Only unmanned spacecraft will travel to Mars.

   H NASA investigators will call for a ban on expeditions to Mars in the future.

   J Scientists will continue to investigate the possibility that life existed on Mars.

13 In addition to learning if there has ever been life on Mars, scientists also wanted to know whether the atmosphere on Mars has ever contained

   A dust

   B gases

   C water

   D nitrogen

© The Continental Press, Inc.   Do not duplicate.

Lesson 7

Revising

When you write a composition, all of the parts of the composition should work together to explain a main idea and show how you think or feel about the topic.

Organization Organization is the way the sentences and paragraphs are put together in a piece of writing. The sentences and paragraphs need to be organized in a logical sequence so the main idea makes sense to the reader and so the reader can follow the writer's argument or discussion. Organization is also important in making sure that the details and examples are presented in a way that supports and helps explain the main idea. If you start out with one main idea, you should go on to explain that idea and use evidence to support it.

Tone The tone of a writing shows how the writer thinks or feels about the topic. You should select the tone for your writing based on the type of writing, your audience (your readers), and your purpose for writing. A letter to the editor protesting the passage of new legislation will have a different tone from a humorous personal essay. Your tone should be intentional and appropriate for your audience and should remain the same throughout the writing.

Diction Diction is the word choice or language you use in the writing. The diction and the way you put sentences together create the tone. As with the tone, the diction should be appropriate for the audience. The diction should also be consistent. If you are writing a letter to a friend, for example, your diction might be very casual. You might use slang words or words that have special meanings to you and your friends. However, if you wrote one sentence in very formal language, that sentence would appear strange and would not fit in with the rest of your letter.

As you put the pieces together to create your composition, your primary focus should be on the main idea. All of the sentences and paragraphs should work together, too. When all of the sentences and paragraphs are organized logically, and the tone and diction are appropriate and consistent, your composition will have clarity. This means it will make sense, the ideas will be clear and easy for the reader to follow, the tone will support and enhance the meaning, and the diction will both support the meaning and make the writing more interesting to read.

© The Continental Press, Inc.   Do not duplicate.

Revising

This indicator focuses on your ability to revise an essay after you have written it. Very few writers can write a clear, consistent essay on the first try. Most writers write at least one rough draft, which they revise. Revising is the process of adding, taking away, or substituting words, phrases, sentences, or paragraphs in order to improve your writing.

Your rough draft may need revising in order to:

- sequence the ideas in a logical way

- develop the ideas

- make sure that there are enough supporting details and examples

- improve the diction or make the diction consistent

- create an appropriate tone or make the tone consistent

- enhance the clarity of the writing

When you review your own rough draft prior to revising, think about these questions:

- What is the main idea or thesis statement?

- What evidence do I use to support the main idea?

- Is the supporting evidence sufficient?

- Are the paragraphs presented in a logical sequence?

- Are there any sentences that seem out of place?

- Are there smooth transitions from paragraph to paragraph?

- What is the tone?

- Is the tone appropriate for my audience?

- What kinds of words or language do I use?

- Is the diction appropriate for my audience?

© The Continental Press, Inc.   Do not duplicate.

Before handing in your composition, you will also want to check your writing to make sure it is complete and correct. Always check your writing for mistakes in grammar, spelling, capitalization, and punctuation. On a test, it may be difficult to check for mistakes in spelling without a dictionary, but sometimes you can figure out how to spell a word by sounding it out.

Guided Practice

Read the paragraph about roller coasters and answer the questions.

Roller coasters are based on physics. The first roller coasters were made of wood. You can learn about physics from roller coasters. First, roller coasters are powered by gravity. That's why the first climb is always very high. The longer the first drop, the more momentum there is to create a long, fast ride. At the bottom of the drop, you feel as if something heavy is pressing you into the seat. That's because, for a moment, you feel several times your actual weight. Have you ever wondered why you don't fall out when you careen into an upside-down loop? The speed at the top of the loop produces twice the normal force of gravity, which means that the force pushing you back into your seat is greater than the force trying to pull you out. What about that feeling when you plunge, and you feel as if your stomach is left back at the top?

Which sentence should be removed from the paragraph?

  A   Roller coasters are based on physics.

  B   The first roller coasters were made of wood.

  C   First, roller coasters are powered by gravity.

  D   The longer the first drop, the more momentum there is to create a long, fast ride.

When you review all of the possible answers, you can see that choice B is the only answer that does not make any reference to the science of roller coasters, so B is the correct answer.

Unit 2 Writing Compositions

© The Continental Press, Inc.   Do not duplicate.

Which of these sentences would be the most effective opening for this paragraph?

    F   The first roller coasters were built in Russia in the 15th century and were actually sleds that slid down icy ramps from the tops of high towers.

    G   You can apply various laws of physics to different kinds of recreational activities.

    H   Roller coasters are frequently named after animals, mythical creatures, and natural phenomena.

    J   Riding a roller coaster may be more fun than reading your physics textbook, but it can be just as educational.

> You can tell that choices F and H are incorrect because they are facts about roller coasters but do not refer to science or physics. Choice G seems possible, but when you compare it to choice J, you see that choice J is the best answer. The opening to a paragraph needs to interest the reader and tell the reader what is to come in the paragraph. Only choice J does both.

Which of these sentences should be added to the end of the paragraph?

    A   That feeling is due to inertia, which is a law of physics that says that bodies tend to resist changes in motion.

    B   People all around the world love to ride on roller coasters and other rides that travel at high speeds.

    C   Riding in a roller coaster can be risky for people with certain health conditions.

    D   Some early American roller coasters were similar to trains and ran on wooden tracks.

> When you skim the answer choices, you can see that answer choices B, C, and D give random facts about roller coasters that do not relate to the end of the paragraph. Choice A is the best answer because it answers the question that was the last sentence of the paragraph.

© The Continental Press, Inc.   Do not duplicate.

Now read this paragraph and answer the questions.

When famous talk show host and producer Oprah Winfrey was a child, she was eager to tell about the kind of job she wanted someday; she wanted to get "paid to talk." This was no small ambition, but Winfrey was no ordinary talker. Her verbal ability won her a college scholarship and a recommendation for her first job. After she relocated to Chicago, Winfrey went on to build a business empire, an empire founded on nothing more than her talent for talking. On her daily television show, Winfrey and her guests talk about everything, from family successes and struggles to shocking medical problems and controversial social issues. Winfrey's success on her show led to her becoming an acclaimed movie and television producer.

Which phrase is the **best** replacement for the underlined phrase in the first sentence?

    F   chatty about what she liked to do

    G   candid about her ambition

    H   not evasive about what she eventually wanted to do

    J   Best as it is

When you read all of the possible answer choices, you can see that all but choice G are unsuitable. Choice F is imprecise, and choice H is too long and wordy. Only choice G fits.

When the author admires Winfrey's "verbal ability," the author means that Winfrey is talented in the way she

    A   uses words to express herself

    B   takes advantage of good opportunities

    C   manages her business

    D   chooses movie and television projects

Oprah Winfrey is probably talented in all of the ways described in the possible answers. But when you go back to look at the phrase "verbal ability" in the context of the paragraph, you see that Winfrey's "verbal ability won her a college scholarship," which has nothing to do with taking advantage of good opportunities (choice B) or her later career as a businesswoman and producer (choices C and D). So choice A is the correct answer.

Unit 2 Writing Compositions

© The Continental Press, Inc.   Do not duplicate.

Which of these words best expresses the meaning of the word *acclaimed* in the last sentence?

F interesting   H talkative

G ambitious   J renowned

> This is similar to a vocabulary question, so you should look back at the word *acclaimed* in context. The sentence has to do with Winfrey's success, which makes choice J the only possible answer.

Here is a rough draft of a student's report about becoming a citizen. Read the rough draft and answer the questions.

---

¹   When an immigrant wants to become a citizen, he or she must become a "legal permanent resident." This means the person can hang out in the United States. Before an immigrant can apply for citizenship, he or she must be at least 18 years old and must live in the United States for five years as a legal permanent resident.

²   People born in the United States are automatically citizens. But some people come to the United States from other countries. They may be immigrants, or residents, but they are not citizens. An immigrant is a guy who the United States lets live here, but this guy doesn't get to do all the things citizens get to do. An immigrant must apply to be a citizen and must meet certain requirements.

³   Many immigrants come to the United States seeking a better life for themselves and their families. A lot of immigrants live in California, Arizona, New Mexico, and Texas. Most people who come to the United States want to be citizens. They want their children to be citizens. They may want the right to vote, which is granted only to citizens. Immigrants are not permitted to vote or to hold public office.

Which would be the best way to order the paragraphs?

A 2, 1, 3   C 3, 1, 2

B 2, 3, 1   D Best as it is

> The paragraphs in the draft are disconnected and out of order. Paragraph 2 gives the main idea and should go first. Paragraph 3 should be second, because it expands on the information in Paragraph 2. Paragraph 1 expands on the information in Paragraph 3, so it should be last. Choice B is correct.

Unit 2 Writing Compositions

99

Which would be the best way to write the underlined phrase in Paragraph 1?

    F stay

    G become a fixture

    H kick it

    J Best as it is

Choice H is slang, so it is too casual in tone and does not fit in with the rest of the essay. Choice G does not match because it is too formal, so it is not consistent with the rest of the essay. Choice F is the only answer that is clear and consistent with the tone of the rest of the essay.

Which would be the best way to write the underlined sentence in Paragraph 2?

    A An immigrant can live in the United States, but can't do some stuff citizens can do and doesn't have to do other stuff citizens have to do.

    B An immigrant is a being who is legally permitted to reside as a resident of the United States, but does not have access to the privileges the United States accords its citizens, nor is he bound to the same responsibilities.

    C An immigrant is a person who is allowed to live in the United States but who does not have the same rights and responsibilities as a citizen.

    D Best as it is

You can tell that choices A and D are too casual in tone and do not match the rest of the essay. Choice B does not match because it is too formal in tone; it also contains unnecessary, repetitive words. Choice C is the only answer that is clear, concise, and consistent with the paragraph.

Which sentence should be added to the beginning of Paragraph 2?

    F Not everyone who lives in the United States is a citizen.

    G People who are born citizens are lucky because they do not have to take a test.

    H Sometimes American citizens are also citizens of another country.

    J Becoming a citizen is not a difficult process, but it does have some important requirements.

Only choice F creates a smooth transition by referring to information in both Paragraph 1 and Paragraph 2, so it is the correct answer.

© The Continental Press, Inc. Do not duplicate.

Which sentence should be removed from Paragraph 3?

    A A lot of immigrants live in California, Arizona, New Mexico, and Texas.

    B Most people who come to the United States want to be citizens.

    C They want their children to be citizens.

    D They may want the right to vote, which is granted only to citizens.

> When you review all of the possible answers, you can see that only choice A strays from the main idea of the paragraph. The paragraph is about why immigrants want to be citizens, but the sentence in choice A focuses on where many immigrants choose to live.

Test Yourself

Read the rough draft of a student report about Aaron Burr. Then answer Numbers 1 through 5.

> Aaron Burr was one of America's worst villains. In 1804, he killed Alexander Hamilton in a duel. Two years later, Burr was involved in a secret plot. He is believed to have been trying to get some states to split off from the rest of the country. Although Burr was arrested and tried for treason, a court found him not guilty of the charges. Burr must have had some good qualities, as he served one term as vice-president and was nearly elected president of the United States. He fought bravely in the Revolutionary War. Burr and Hamilton were sometimes rivals in the courtroom.
>
> Like many politicians today, Burr was a lawyer by profession; he was one of the best lawyers in New York City, both before and after his career in politics. Obviously, New Yorkers didn't mind if their lawyers had committed a crime or two.

1 Which sentence does not fit well in the first paragraph?

    A Aaron Burr was one of America's worst villains.

    B Burr and Hamilton were sometimes rivals in the courtroom.

    C Although Burr was arrested and tried for treason, a court found him not guilty of the charges.

    D He fought bravely in the Revolutionary War.

© The Continental Press, Inc.   Do not duplicate.

2 Which phrase is the <u>best</u> replacement for the underlined phrase in the first sentence?

   F horrid monsters

   G infamous actors

   H most unfriendly people

   J Best as it is

3 Which fact <u>best</u> supports the idea that Aaron Burr was a villain?

   A He was a successful attorney in New York City.

   B He served a term as vice-president of the United States.

   C He killed Alexander Hamilton in a duel.

   D He fought in the Revolutionary War.

4 Which of these words <u>best</u> expresses the meaning of the word *rivals* in the last sentence of the first paragraph?

   F enemies

   G lawyers

   H competitors

   J candidates

5 Which would be the <u>best</u> way to write the underlined sentence?

   A People gossiped that maybe there was a plot in which he might have been involved that was about getting some states to pull out of the United States.

   B It is thought that Burr may have participated in the leadership of an attempt to persuade certain states to separate themselves from the rest of the states in the United States.

   C Burr was suspected of instigating several states to secede from the United States.

   D Best as it is

© The Continental Press, Inc.   Do not duplicate.

Read the rough draft of a student report about keeping pet snakes. Then answer Numbers 6 through 12.

1   When choosing a pet, you have to consider the pet's needs for shelter, food, and even entertainment. The needs of some animals, such as dogs and cats, can be met in a relatively convenient way, since they do not usually need a separate cage. Most dogs and cats will eat pet food that is available at any pet store. If you choose an unusual pet, like a snake, you are entering a different world. But snakes are cool pets anyway, because they scare people.

2   There are many things to consider about a pet snake. The most important consideration is whether you can make the long-term commitment to caring for a snake, including providing a safe, healthy habitat that meets your pet's needs. Snakes are particular about their habitats. Snakes need a lot of room; a snake needs about 3/4 square foot of space for each 12 inches of its length. In addition, snakes need plenty of fresh air, but their enclosure must be escape-proof. Such enclosures may be expensive and can cost hundreds of dollars, depending on the size and the materials used. You must also be able to maintain the right temperature. Some snakes need a constant temperature of between 80 and 90 degrees Fahrenheit. This might sound fine for the summer, but are you willing to pay the extra hike in your winter heating bills? And it should go without saying that the snake's home needs to be kept clean in order for the snake to remain healthy.

3   Diet is important to a snake's health, too. As with temperatures, different snakes have different dietary requirements and preferences. A snake that is not offered the right kind of food might not eat even if the snake is very hungry. Be especially careful with live food, such as rats; a snake that is not hungry might end up being dinner for your new pet rat.

© The Continental Press, Inc.   Do not duplicate.

6 Which sentence should be removed from Paragraph 1?

    F When choosing a pet, you have to consider the pet's needs for shelter, food, and even entertainment.

    G The needs of some animals, such as dogs and cats, can be met in a relatively convenient way, since they do not usually need a separate cage and may eat commercially available pet food.

    H If you choose an unusual pet, like a snake, you are entering a different world.

    J But snakes are cool pets anyway, because they scare people.

7 Which would be the best way to write the underlined sentence?

    A Choosing an unusual pet, like a snake, requires more thought and commitment from an owner.

    B A snake is an unusual pet; it lives in a different world.

    C It is thought that snakes are hard pets to take care of.

    D Best as it is

8 Which of these words is the best replacement for the underlined word in Paragraph 2?

    F objects

    G issues

    H tasks

    J diets

9 Which would be the best way to write the underlined phrase in Paragraph 3?

    A a sacrifice to the hunger of

    B getting wolfed down by

    C becoming consumed and digested by

    D Best as it is

10 Suppose you are writing a fourth paragraph for this rough draft. The topic of the paragraph should be

    F how to build a reptile enclosure

    G why snakes make good pets

    H habitats of rats and mice

    J entertainment for snakes

Unit 2 Writing Compositions

© The Continental Press, Inc.   Do not duplicate.

11 Which sentence **best** supports the idea that people who keep other kinds of pets have an easier time meeting their pet's needs compared to snake owners?

    A The needs of some animals, such as dogs and cats, can be met in a relatively convenient way, as they do not usually need a separate cage and may eat commercially available pet food.

    B The most important consideration is whether you can make the long-term commitment to caring for a snake, including providing a safe, healthy habitat that meets your pet's needs.

    C Snakes need a lot of room; a snake needs about 3/4 square foot of space for each 12 inches of its length.

    D Be especially careful with live food, such as rats; a snake that is not hungry might end up being dinner for your new pet rat.

12 Which would be the **best** way to order the paragraphs?

    F 2, 3, 1

    G 2, 1, 3

    H 3, 2, 1

    J Best as it is

© The Continental Press, Inc.   Do not duplicate.

USING LANGUAGE

Language is a tool that you use in many ways every day as you speak, read, and write. To use language effectively, you need to apply the conventions of Standard English. You began to learn this from the time you moved out of the "baby talk" stage of saying, "Me want milk" to saying, "I'd like a glass of milk." This is an example of using good grammar, which is one of the conventions of Standard English that is important in speaking and writing. There are other conventions that are important in writing, such as spelling, capitalization, punctuation, and word usage. Good writers learn how to edit and proofread their work for these conventions. The goal of this unit is that you will demonstrate the ability to control language by applying the conventions of Standard English in your writing.

Lesson 1

Language Usage

Vocabulary is the key to reading and writing. In order to understand what you are reading, you must know the meaning of the words. You probably have a larger vocabulary than you think. Most people have a vocabulary of more than 15,000 words. Those are the words you recognize when you hear or read them. You also use context clues (the words and phrases near an unfamiliar word) to figure out the meaning of a word you don't know.

3.2.1 The student will choose the level of language, formal to informal, appropriate for a specific audience, situation, or purpose.

Levels of Language

This indicator focuses on your ability to understand different levels of language and choose the right language for a specific purpose. Many words have more than one level of meaning. The word *earth* is an example. In an informational article about the Mir space station, the word *Earth* would be used literally to refer to the planet we live on. In a literary passage, such as an excerpt from the novel *The Good Earth*, however, the word *earth* has a different literal meaning; then it means land for planting crops. There is also a symbolic meaning to the word *earth* in the novel. *Earth* suggests the land as the source of life.

© The Continental Press, Inc.   Do not duplicate.

Vocabulary questions on a test often ask about the meaning of a word or phrase in a reading passage or sentence. You may need to read the word and its context more than once to figure out its meaning. If the question doesn't give you enough context, reread the paragraph from the passage that contains the word or phrase.

The easiest way to increase your vocabulary is by reading.	People who read learn more words just by reading. As you read, you usually guess what a word means from context. After you see it a few times, the word becomes part of your vocabulary. It's always a good idea to look up a new word in the dictionary. You might be surprised at what the word really means. For example, do you really know the meaning of *elementary?*

3.2.2 The student will differentiate connotative from denotative meanings of words.

3.2.3 The student will describe how readers or listeners might respond differently to the same words.

Denotative and Connotative Meanings

The **denotative** meaning of a word is its literal meaning (Earth = our planet). The denotative meaning is the object or quality that the word stands for. For example, in the sentence "You can sit in that chair," the word *chair* simply means a piece of furniture. The word *chair* does not imply any other meaning or feeling.

An author may also use a word or phrase to suggest an idea. That is the word's **connotative** meaning (earth = the source of life). You can see from the two examples of the way *earth* is used that readers might respond differently to the same word used in a different context. Connotative language is a kind of shortcut to imply something that is not stated. This implied meaning adds to the descriptive power of the word or phrase. For example, in the sentence "You can sit at the head of the table," the phrase *head of the table* carries a connotation that this is the place of honor or authority, and sitting there is a privilege.

Connotative language is also used to set a mood or to encourage specific feelings in the reader. For example, if a character is described as having the "rolling gait of a sailor," the word *rolling* is connotative and, coupled with the image of a sailor, adds the idea of the motion of the sea. You can imagine the character's walk by picturing a sailor moving about on the deck of a ship tossed by the waves.

© The Continental Press, Inc.   Do not duplicate.

Guided Practice

Now read and answer these questions.

Read the following sentences.

> I opened the door at the end of the dark hallway to see a tiny room, cozy and snug—a rocking chair, a desk, and a bed with a soft, blue blanket. This would be my home for the next four years.

In this sentence, the words *cozy* and *snug* suggest a sense of

    A cold

    B tightness

    C leisure

    D comfort

If you didn't know what "cozy" and "snug" mean, you would look back at the context of the sentences for more clues. "A soft, blue blanket," a "rocking chair," and the word "home" suggest a pleasant, relaxed place, so choices C and D are both possibilities. "Cozy" has a connotation of being warm and comfortable. "Snug" can mean "tight," but since it is used with "cozy," you can tell that the word "comfort," choice D, fits best.

Read the following sentence.

> The interior of the artist's home presents a crazy-quilt of color, a tumultuous jumble of riotous hues.

The words *crazy-quilt, tumultuous,* and *riotous* suggest an atmosphere of

    F quiet calm

    G restrained creativity

    H joyful chaos

    J luxurious abundance

First, try to picture the room as it is described in the sentence. Then look at all the answer choices. You can rule out choices F and G because you know that the atmosphere is not quiet or restrained if it is "tumultuous" and "riotous." There is nothing in the sentence to make you think that choice J is correct. The context—the other words in the sentence, such as "crazy quilt of color"—tells you that choice H is the only answer that fits.

© The Continental Press, Inc.   Do not duplicate.

Read the following sentence.

> When Uncle Ned came into the kitchen, Champ shrank into the corner, his tail between his legs.

In this sentence, the connotation of the word *shrank* suggests that Champ is

    A smaller

    B creeping

    C friendly

    D frightened

Champ doesn't seem to be friendly, so answer C is not what you are looking for. *Shrank* does mean to have gotten smaller, but since Champ is a dog, that is not likely. Champ could be creeping, answer B, but that is a literal interpretation. By using the word *shrank* to describe the dog's action, the author is suggesting that Champ is afraid of Uncle Ned. Another clue is that Champ has his tail between his legs, a sign that the dog is frightened. Choice D is the correct answer.

Test Yourself

Read the excerpt from a story. Then answer Numbers 1 through 4.

> At night Lena's father would enchant her with hypnotic stories from his own childhood, tales of that distant country across the faraway sea. Her father told legends of noble heroes on righteous quests, kings and queens dispensing justice, warrior princesses and honorable deeds. After each story, he would remind her, "These stories are all the gold I have to give you. These stories are your inheritance."

1 **In the first sentence, the words *enchant* and *hypnotic* show that**

    A Lena became completely absorbed by the stories

    B Lena fell asleep when she heard the stories

    C Lena's father had studied magic

    D Lena's father told the stories with a certain rhythm

2 **In the second sentence, the words *righteous*, *honorable*, and *justice* suggest that the characters in the stories are**

    F brave

    G royal

    H powerful

    J virtuous

© The Continental Press, Inc.   Do not duplicate.

3 The words *tales* and *legends* suggest that the stories

    A have been told for many years

    B will have a surprise ending

    C are about her father's life

    D are meant for children

4 What does Lena's father mean when he tells her that his stories are "gold" and that they are her "inheritance"?

    F He is too poor to give her money.

    G The messages of the stories are valuable.

    H She can write the stories down and sell them.

    J The stories will lead her to great wealth.

© The Continental Press, Inc.   Do not duplicate.

Lesson 2

Grammar

Grammar refers to the way words are put together to form sentences. Some sentences are very simple—a declarative statement, such as "I read that book" or "She went home." A simple question can be a complete sentence: "Where are you?" or even "What happened?" Other sentences are more complex. They are created by putting together groups of words, or clauses. You can even put together two complete sentences to make a new sentence.

Because you speak, read, and write English every day, you probably know more about grammar than you realize. If a sentence sounds strange or doesn't make sense, it probably has some kind of mistake. For example, we usually put the subject of the sentence before the verb and object. The sentence "To the store we are going" sounds strange to us; the correct way to write the sentence is "We are going to the store." If a sentence does not make sense when you read it, the sentence is probably written incorrectly.

3.1.3 The student will explain how words are classified grammatically by meaning, position, form, and function.

Parts of Speech

This indicator requires you to understand and correctly use various parts of speech, or grammatical classifications. These include nouns, pronouns, verbs, adjectives, adverbs, prepositions, conjunctions, and transition words. It also includes the subject, predicate, and object in a sentence.

Nouns

A noun is the name of a person, place, or thing. Here are some nouns:

government	apartment
knowledge	cake
tree	game
family	bicycle

In this sentence, the words *book* and *shelf* are both nouns.

The <u>book</u> is on the <u>shelf</u>.

There are several ways to tell if a word is a noun. One way is that it often comes after an **article** (the words *a, an,* or *the*).

The <u>cat</u> jumped to the top of <u>the fence</u>.

<u>An elephant</u> led <u>the parade</u>.

© The Continental Press, Inc.   Do not duplicate.

Another way to tell if a word is a noun is that nouns can often be plural. That is, there can be more than one. Here are some plural nouns:

cats	ideas
mice	apples
geese	voters

Some nouns can be made out of other words by adding certain suffixes or endings.

WORD	SUFFIX	NOUN
govern	-ment	government
state		statement
settle		settlement
add	-tion or -sion	addition
permit		permission
discuss		discussion
read	-er	reader
write		writer
play		player

Another way to tell if a word is a noun is that it can be a subject or an object in a sentence. The subject is the person or thing in a sentence that performs the action. You can say that the subject is the "doer" in the sentence. The object is the recipient of the action. Look at this sentence:

Mike hit the ball.

In this sentence, you can tell that *Mike* is the subject because he is doing the action. The *ball* is the object because it is receiving the action. Both are nouns.

Sometimes nouns function as **adjectives.** This means that nouns can be used to describe other nouns.

The coach wants us to be team players.

Usually the word *team* is a noun. In this sentence, it is used as an adjective because it is used to describe a certain kind of player.

Pronouns

Pronouns are words that stand for nouns. We use different forms of pronouns, depending on whether the pronoun is the subject or the object of a sentence. Remember that the subject is the person or thing that performs an action in a sentence. Here are the pronouns we use when the pronoun is the subject: *I, you, he, she, it, we, they.*

Unit 3 Using Language

© The Continental Press, Inc.   Do not duplicate.

In these sentences, the pronouns are the subjects:

> She works with a nature preservation organization.

> We explored a new part of the city yesterday.

> They just became interested in the sport of spelunking.

When the pronoun is the object of a sentence (the thing that is acted upon), the form of the pronoun can change. Here are the pronouns we use when the pronoun is the object of the sentence: *me, you, him, her, it, us, them.*

In these sentences, the pronouns are the objects:

> Did you help him wash the car?

> I invited her to join our study group.

This is also the form of the pronoun to use when the pronoun is the object of a preposition. A **preposition** is a word that is put in front of a noun or pronoun to make a prepositional phrase. A prepositional phrase modifies another word in the sentence. Here are some common prepositions:

about	as	between	for
above	at	beyond	from
across	before	but	in
after	behind	by	near
against	below	down	next
around	beside	during	of

In these sentences, the pronouns are the objects of prepositions:

> I stopped to visit with them.

> Did you want to buy a gift for him?

The words *as* and *than* are prepositions. When you use a pronoun in a comparison containing prepositions such as *than* or *as,* you choose a different form of the pronoun, depending on what you want to say. Here is one example:

> She likes social studies better than me.

The choice of *me* is fine if I intend to say that she likes social studies better than she likes me. What I probably meant to say was that she likes social studies better *than I do.* It is simple to choose a pronoun in this kind of phrase if you think about the meaning of the rest of the sentence. Here are some examples:

> Eva is better at public speaking than I [am].

> No one can run as fast as he [can].

> Jeff thinks my brother is better at golf than [he thinks] I [am].

© The Continental Press, Inc.   Do not duplicate.

The words *who* and *whom* are pronouns, just like *he* and *him*. Your choice of pronoun depends on the sentence and what you are trying to say. Just as with other pronouns, you can decide whether to use *who* or *whom* by figuring out whether the pronoun is the subject (the person doing the action of a clause or sentence) or the object (the person who is acted upon in a clause or sentence). *Who* is used as the subject of a sentence. As with the pronouns *him*, *her*, and *them*, *whom* is used as an object of an action. *Whom* is also used as the object of a preposition.

In these sentences, *who* is the subject:

Who was elected class treasurer? (*Who* is the subject of the sentence.)

Kelly, who always looks like she is asleep, surprised the teacher with the right answer. (*Who* is the subject of the clause.)

In these sentences, *whom* is the object:

To whom does this sweater belong? (*Whom* is the object of the preposition *to*.)

The new student, whom we all like, is from South America. (*Whom* is the object of the verb *like*.)

Verbs

You know that a **verb** is an action word. This means that it shows the action of a sentence. Here are some examples of verbs:

go

think

wander

anticipate

celebrate

However, sometimes a verb has a different function in a sentence. A verb can function as an adjective, an adverb, or even a noun. A verb that is functioning as another part of speech is called a verbal, or is part of a verbal phrase.

Here are some different forms of verbs:

• infinitive: to walk, to go, to see

• present participle: walking, going, seeing

• past participle: walked, gone, seen

Here are some sentences that contain verbals and verbal phrases:

A well-fed cat is a happy cat.

Wearing the school T-shirt is one way we show school spirit on Fridays.

We spent the summer swimming at the lake and hiking in the mountains.

© The Continental Press, Inc.   Do not duplicate.

Adjectives and Adverbs

Adverbs are words that are used to modify verbs. Adverbs describe *where, when, how,* or *how often* an action is performed. Adverbs can also modify adjectives or other adverbs.

A common mistake is to use **adjectives** (words that modify nouns) instead of adverbs.

Here is a sentence that shows this mistake:

The band played so <u>loud</u> I couldn't hear the next day.

In the above sentence, the adjective *loud* should be replaced by the adverb *loudly:*

The band played so <u>loudly</u> I couldn't hear the next day.

An adverb should be used to describe a verb (any kind of action).

On the other hand, adjectives, such as *kind, intelligent,* or *colorful,* are used to describe nouns (people, places, things, or even ideas):

That band was <u>great</u>.

But if you wanted to talk about how the band played music, you would use an adjective instead of an adverb:

That band played <u>well</u>.

Conjunctions and Transitions

Conjunctions are words used to link clauses in a sentence. Different conjunctions may be used to create different meanings. The conjunction *but* is used to show contrast, as in this sentence:

I voted for Dave for class president, <u>but</u> I was in the minority.

Transitions take the reader from one sentence or idea to another. Some transitions are phrases, such as *for example, after all, in addition,* and *on the contrary.* Other transitions are conjunctions that are also adverbs, because they modify the verb: *similarly, still, also, otherwise, instead, meanwhile, however,* etc. Here are some ways transitions are used:

- to give examples (for instance, in fact, for example)
- to add information (and, in addition, besides, furthermore)
- to compare (likewise, also, similarly)
- to contrast (but, however, although, even though)
- to show a connection (as a result, thus, therefore, since)
- to show time or place (after, finally, beyond, nearby)

Here is a sentence with a transition that shows contrast:

Today's forecast calls for rain; <u>however</u>, there is not a cloud in the sky.

© The Continental Press, Inc.   Do not duplicate.

When deciding which transition to use, think first about your purpose. You may want to show similarities or differences. You may want to show a logical connection. Maybe you just want to add information to what you have already said. When you are clear in your purpose, you will choose a transition that will make your writing clear and easy to follow.

Guided Practice

Answer the three questions that follow.

Read the sentence.

> One day, while flying over a rural area in a hot-air balloon, a man realized that he was lost.

Which of these words is <u>not</u> used as a verb in this sentence?

    A lost

    B flying

    C realized

    D was

Think about what you know about verbs. A verb is an action word. "Flying" is used as the gerund, or the *–ing* form of the verb *fly,* so choice B is not the answer. Both "realized" and "was" are past tense forms of verbs, so choices C and D are not possible answers. Choice A, "lost," which functions in this sentence as an adjective, is correct.

Read the sentence.

> At the mill, the cotton is cleaned again, then formed into rolls like giant spools of thread.

Which of these words is used as a verb in this sentence?

    F rolls

    G spools

    H thread

    J formed

This question may seem tricky at first, because all of these words can be used as verbs. Review the sentence to make sure you understand how each word is functioning in the sentence. "Rolls," "spools," and "thread" are all used as nouns. Only choice J, the word "formed," is used as a verb.

© The Continental Press, Inc.   Do not duplicate.

Read the sentence.

> Then alphabets and writing systems were developed with the purpose of recording information to share with others.

Which of these is the <u>subject</u> of the sentence?

    A purpose

    B others

    C recording information

    D alphabets and writing systems

You know that the subject of a sentence is the part of the sentence that performs the action. Look at the sentence again. Which word or words perform the action of the sentence? One way to find out if a word or phrase is the subject is to try removing that word or phrase from the sentence. If the words that are left do not make a sentence, the word or phrase you removed may be the subject. In this sentence, "alphabets and writing systems" are the subject, and choice D is correct.

Avoiding Errors in Grammar

Errors in grammar may include mistakes in the way verbs, pronouns, and other parts of speech are used.

Here is an example of a sentence with grammatical mistakes in the way pronouns are used:

    Me and her went for a walk.

The pronouns *me* and *her* should only be used as objects in a sentence, rather than as the subjects of a sentence. You can fix this sentence by replacing the incorrect pronouns *me* and *her* with the correct pronouns *I* and *she* and then by reversing the order in which they appear. The correct way to write this sentence is:

    She and I went for a walk.

Mistakes in using nouns may include subject-verb agreement. The noun that is the subject of a sentence must agree with the verb in number. Can you see the mistake in this sentence?

    Kia and Alex likes to travel.

The subject (Kia and Alex) is plural, but the singular form (likes) of the verb *like* is used. Here is the correct way to write this sentence:

    Kia and Alex like to travel.

The verb tense must also be correct. For example, if you are talking about something that will happen in the future, you would use the future tense of the verb:

    I <u>will vote</u> in the next presidential election.

© The Continental Press, Inc.   Do not duplicate.

3.1.5 The student will incorporate subjects, predicates, and modifiers when composing original sentences.

3.1.6 The student will compound various sentence elements—subjects, predicates, modifiers, phrases, and clauses—to link or contrast related ideas.

Clauses

These indicators focus on using various parts of speech and sentence elements to compose sentences. Every simple sentence is a clause because a clause has a subject (a noun or pronoun) and a predicate (a verb). Not every clause is a sentence, though. A subordinate clause, one that begins with a word such as *when*, *since*, *because*, or *although*, cannot stand alone as a sentence.

Greg began surfing when he was ten years old.

Look for the subject and the predicate in each clause. Notice that the main clause *Greg began surfing* is a complete sentence that tells you what Greg did. The second (or subordinate) clause, *when he was ten years old*, is not a complete sentence because it doesn't tell you anything.

Phrases

There are several kinds of phrases. **Prepositional phrases** are the simplest; they include a preposition and a noun and often some modifying words.

We went for a long walk.

For a long walk is a prepositional phrase. There is no subject and no predicate. Prepositional phrases are like adjectives and adverbs. They add descriptive information.

Here is an example of a **gerund phrase**:

Walking along the beach is my favorite activity.

Gerunds are words that end in *-ing*. A gerund phrase is like a noun; it can be the subject of a sentence or the object. The subject of this sentence is the gerund phrase *walking along the beach*.

Here is an **infinitive phrase**:

I like to walk along the beach.

Infinitives are verbs with *to:* (to walk, to sing, to complain.) An infinitive phrase is also like a noun and can be used as the subject of a sentence or the object. In this sentence, the infinitive phrase *to walk along the beach* is the object of the sentence.

© The Continental Press, Inc.   Do not duplicate.

Participial phrases look like gerunds, but they function like adjectives and adverbs:

> Walking along the beach, Greg wished he could surf.

In this sentence, *walking along the beach* is a participial phrase because it modifies a noun, the name *Greg.* Adjectives modify nouns.

On a test, you might be asked to correct a sentence that contains a misplaced phrase or clause. Here is an example of a sentence with a misplaced participial phrase:

> Clarissa saw a deer driving home from work.

Obviously this is wrong because it doesn't make sense. It sounds as if the deer is driving home from work. The mistake is that the participial phrase, *driving home from work,* is not next to the word it modifies, *Clarissa.* The sentence should be rewritten like this:

> Driving home from work, Clarissa saw a deer.

Modifying words, phrases, and clauses should usually be close to the word they modify. This sentence is awkward and hard to understand:

> The price of computers is coming down, for laptops.

The sentence can be rewritten so that it is easier to read and understand by putting the word that refers to computers next to it.

> The price of laptop computers is coming down.

When you write sentences with more than one phrase, you must use the same kind of phrase. Here is an example of a sentence with phrases that are not the same:

> Greg likes walking along the beach and to surf.

You can probably figure out that the sentence should be written one of these two ways:

> Greg likes walking along the beach and surfing.

> OR

> Greg likes to walk along the beach and to surf.

© The Continental Press, Inc.   Do not duplicate.

Guided Practice

For the following two questions, choose the answer that is the most effective substitute for the underlined part of the sentence. If the sentence is correct, choose "Best as it is."

<u>Working at a fast food restaurant</u>, French fries are a real temptation.

    A Working at a fast food restaurant, anyone is tempted by the French fries.

    B When you work at a fast food restaurant, French fries are a real temptation.

    C French fries are a real temptation working at a fast food restaurant.

    D Best as it is

The sentence doesn't make sense because it doesn't suggest that a person works at a fast food restaurant or is tempted by the French fries. Choices A and B both provide that information, but choice B makes more sense, so B is the right answer.

We need help shopping and <u>to prepare food</u> for the party.

    F To prepare food, we need help shopping for the party.

    G Help was needed to shop and preparing food for the party.

    H We need help shopping and preparing food for the party.

    J Best as it is

This sentence mixes a gerund phrase and an infinitive phrase. Choices F and G do not fix the problem. Only choice H uses two gerunds—*shopping* and *preparing*.

3.1.4 The student will differentiate grammatically complete sentences from non-sentences.

Complete Sentences

In order to answer many test questions, you must be able to identify a complete sentence. A sentence always has a subject and a predicate. The subject is a noun or pronoun; the predicate is a verb. Here is a complete sentence:

The bus stopped.

In this sentence, the subject is *The bus* and the predicate is *stopped*. If more words are added to the sentence, the subject and predicate are the same:

The bright yellow bus stopped in front of the daycare center.

© The Continental Press, Inc. Do not duplicate.

A sentence is not complete without both a subject and predicate. Here are two sentence fragments, or incomplete sentences:

About a dozen small children.

Lined up next to the bus.

These two sentence fragments can be combined to make a complete sentence because the first one has a subject (children) and the second one has a predicate (lined up).

About a dozen small children lined up next to the bus.

Run-on Sentences

A run-on sentence is the opposite of a sentence fragment. It is two or more sentences written as one. Here is an example:

At the library, we did research for our term project, our project is about the tropical rain forest.

You can fix this sentence in several different ways. You can write two sentences.

At the library, we did research for our term project. Our project is about the tropical rain forest.

You can also combine the two sentences into one sentence.

At the library, we did research for our term project, which is about the tropical rain forest.

3.1.7 The student will vary sentence types—simple, compound, complex, and compound/complex—to sustain reader or listener interest.

Varying Sentence Structure

Combining sentences and clauses is a way you can vary the sentence structure in your writing. Write some complicated sentences and some short, simple sentences. If you only use very short, simple sentences, the writing is not as interesting to read. Varying the length and the structure of the sentence will help you keep your writing from sounding dull and repetitive.

© The Continental Press, Inc.   Do not duplicate.

Guided Practice

Answer these questions.

Which of the following is a complete sentence?

 A Carried the kitten in a towel.

 B We brought a towel with us.

 C A tiny gray and white one.

 D Fit in the palm of my hand.

> Although there are nouns in choice A, there is no subject for the predicate (carried), so A is not the right answer. Choice D also has a predicate (fit) but no subject. Choice C has a subject, but no predicate. Only choice B has both a subject (We) and a predicate (brought).

Which is the correct way to write this as a sentence?

> Change a tire on the freeway on his way to work this morning.

 F My dad had to change a tire on the freeway on his way to work this morning.

 G On his way to work this morning, change a tire on the freeway.

 H My dad on his way to work this morning.

 J Best as it is

> Only choice F has both a subject and a predicate, so it is the correct answer. Choice G uses the same words in different order, but there is still no subject. Choice H has a subject, but no predicate.

Which is the correct way to write this as a sentence?

> Salma speaks perfect Spanish, she is fluent in English, too.

 A Salma speaks Spanish perfectly, she speaks English, too.

 B Salma speaks perfect Spanish, and she is fluent in English, too.

 C She is fluent in English, Salma speaks Spanish, too.

 D Best as it is

> This is an example of a run-on sentence. Choices A and C are also run-on sentences, so they cannot be the correct answer. In choice B, the two sentences have been joined into a compound sentence. It is the correct answer.

© The Continental Press, Inc. Do not duplicate.

Test Yourself

Now read these sentences and answer the questions.

1 | It was built more than 2,300 years ago by the Roman army to enable soldiers, pack animals, and supply wagons to move quickly through the empire.

Which of these words is used as a verb in this sentence?

A pack

B enable

C supply

D empire

2 | And what the Romans did with those ideas was to make them work and put them into everyday use.

Which of these words is not used as a verb in this sentence?

F did

G make

H put

J use

3 | Unlike diamonds and sapphires, amber is an "organic" stone and so has unusual properties.

Which of these is the subject of the sentence?

A sapphires

B diamonds

C amber

D properties

4 | The king demanded that his knights bring the treasures to the castle.

Which of these is the object of a preposition?

F king

G knights

H treasures

J castle

Unit 3 Using Language   **123**

© The Continental Press, Inc.   Do not duplicate.

5 | However, the truly remarkable flaw in the plan went unnoticed by the conspirators.

Which word functions as a noun in the sentence?

A   However

B   remarkable

C   unnoticed

D   conspirators

6 | Had to stop at the library on the way home from school today.

Which is the correct way to write this as a sentence?

F   On the way home from school today had to stop at the library.

G   Today on the way home from school had to stop at the library.

H   I had to stop at the library on the way home from school today.

J   Best as it is

7 | Erin likes to draw and paint she also likes to play the piano.

Which is the correct way to write this as a sentence?

A   Erin likes to draw, paint, and play the piano.

B   Erin likes to draw, likes to paint, likes to play the piano.

C   Erin likes to draw she likes to paint she likes to play the piano.

D   Best as it is

8 | Stayed up very late to study, too tired in the morning to do anything.

Which is the correct way to write this as a sentence?

F   Because I stayed up very late to study, I was too tired to do anything in the morning.

G   Too tired in the morning to do anything, because stayed up very late to study.

H   Staying up very late to study means too tired in the morning to do anything.

J   Best as it is

© The Continental Press, Inc.   Do not duplicate.

9 Which of these is a **complete** sentence?

    A Went to the beach.

    B We brought a picnic lunch.

    C High crashing waves at the shore.

    D Stayed all day there.

10

> Helping as an aide in the school office always a coveted job by seniors.

Which is the correct way to write this as a sentence?

    F Helping as an aide in the school office is always a job coveted by seniors.

    G Always a coveted job by seniors, helping as an aide in the school office.

    H Coveted always by seniors the job helping as an aide in the school office.

    J Best as it is

© The Continental Press, Inc.   Do not duplicate.

Lesson 3

Capitalization, Punctuation, and Spelling

It is important to use correct capitalization, punctuation, and spelling in your writing so that what you write can easily be read and understood. After you write a draft, the next step is to edit and proofread your work. Checking your writing for correct capitalization, punctuation, and spelling is part of proofreading. You will learn more about editing and proofreading in Lesson 4.

3.3 The student will use capitalization, punctuation, and correct spelling appropriately.

The focus of this indicator and of this lesson is your ability to use correct capitalization, punctuation, and spelling in your writing. You will notice that this lesson is organized a bit differently from the other lessons in this book. Instead of the exercises in **Guided Practice** and **Test Yourself,** you will find short practice exercises following each section of explanation. Most of these rules of capitalization, punctuation, and spelling will be familiar to you. However, take time to read this lesson carefully and do the practice exercises. It will be a good review, and you just might learn something new!

CAPITALIZATION

Nouns name people, animals, places, and things. A common noun is a general name, like *man* and *river*. A proper noun is a particular name, like *Jack* or *Amazon*. Proper nouns are always capitalized.

- Names of **particular people** are proper nouns. They should be capitalized, including initials and titles of respect or office.

Naguib Mahfouz   Hazel R. O'Leary
President Bush   Aunt Ellen
                 Dr. and Mrs. Victor B. Chavez

Remember that words like *doctor, uncle,* and *senator* are not capitalized unless they are used as titles before names.

Our family doctor is Dr. Robin Miller.

- Names of **particular animals and things** are also proper nouns and should be capitalized.

Shamu   Prairie Bayou   Titanic

© The Continental Press, Inc.   Do not duplicate.

Capitalize the first letter of each proper noun in the sentences below.

1. The names of christopher columbus's ships were the *niña,* the *pinta,* and the *santa maria.*

2. washoe is a chimp that dr. r. fouts taught to use sign language.

3. The concorde was a very fast airplane.

4. roy rogers rode a horse named trigger and had a dog named bullet.

- Names of **particular places** are proper nouns and should be capitalized, too. For example, names of continents and countries are capitalized.

North America   Europe   United States   Spain

- Names of **towns, cities, counties,** and **states** are also capitalized as proper nouns.

El Paso   Montgomery County   North Dakota

- The particular names of **bodies of water** are capitalized as proper nouns. This includes names of **oceans, seas, lakes, rivers, gulfs, bays,** and so on.

Atlantic Ocean   Mississippi River   Gulf of Mexico   Chesapeake Bay

- Specific **areas of land** may also have particular names. Like other place names, the names of **mountains, islands, capes,** and **parks** are proper nouns and should be capitalized.

Cape Cod   Prince Edward Island   Yellowstone National Park

- If **direction words** are part of the name of a specific area or region, they are capitalized as proper nouns.

Israel and Egypt are countries in the Middle East.

- Particular names of **roadways** and **bridges** are proper nouns and should be capitalized.

King Street   Pennsylvania Turnpike   Chesapeake Bay Bridge

- Proper nouns also include names of **buildings** and **special landmarks.** They should be capitalized.

White House   Statue of Liberty   Palace Hotel

- Names of **holidays** and other **special days** are proper nouns and should be capitalized.

Thanksgiving   April Fool's Day   Memorial Day

- Names of **nationalities** are proper nouns. So are names of **religions** and of the groups of people who believe in them. All these proper nouns should be capitalized.

the French   Zen Buddhism   Americans   Baptists

- Particular names of organizations are proper nouns. So, the names of **clubs, teams, companies, stores, parts of government,** and other special groups are capitalized.

Pittsburgh Pirates   Department of Health   Dolly's Diner

© The Continental Press, Inc. Do not duplicate.

- Particular names of **historical** or **special events, periods,** and **documents** are also proper nouns and should be capitalized.

      Roman Empire   Super Bowl   Constitution of the United States

- The first word and all important words in the titles of books, magazines, newspapers, stories, poems, movies, plays, and TV shows are capitalized.

      The Joy Luck Club   People   the Denver Post   "Wild World of Sports"

Rewrite each sentence below, capitalizing words as necessary.

1. The taino indians called puerto rico "land of the noble lord."

    _____

2. mrs. mary chestnut, who was from the south, wrote a diary during america's civil war.

    _____

3. The *spirit of st. louis*, which charles lindbergh flew to france, can still be seen at the smithsonian institution in washington, d.c.

    _____

4. Ian Ian, a giant panda at the ueno zoo in tokyo, was much loved by the japanese.

    _____

5. groundhog greetings, inc., makes greeting cards for all holidays, but especially for groundhog day.

    _____

6. Many new lands were discovered in the age of exploration.

    _____

7. The show *west side story* is based on shakespeare's *romeo and juliet*.

    _____

PUNCTUATION

End Punctuation

Every sentence must end with a punctuation mark. There are three end punctuation marks, the period (.), the question mark (?), and the exclamation point (!)

- A **period** is used to end a sentence that states or tells something.

    Giant pandas are rare animals.
    They live in China.

© The Continental Press, Inc.   Do not duplicate.

A period may also be used to end a command or request.

> Move the chair closer to the lamp.
> Please show me your new house.

- A **question mark** is used to end a sentence that asks something.

> Where is Sean?
> Did you close the door?

- An **exclamation point** is used to end an exclamatory sentence, one that shows surprise or strong feeling.

> What a wonderful present Lee gave me!
> How beautiful it is!

Write the correct punctuation mark at the end of each sentence below.

1. Go see the Westminster Kennel Club dog show

2. It was first held in 1877

3. Does a dog have to be perfect to win

4. In 1980, a husky named Cinnar won even though the top of his ear had been bitten off in a fight

5. How wonderful

6. What a brave dog he turned out to be

Quotation Marks

- **Quotation marks** are used before and after the exact words someone has spoken. Quotation marks come <u>after</u> the end punctuation.

> "Was Mr. Bojangles a real person?" asked Lena.
> Jerome answered, "For sure!"
> Jerome added, "His real name was Bill Robinson."

- A **comma** is used to separate the speaker and verbs such as *said, asked, answered, exclaimed,* and *continued.* If the speaker comes before the quotation, a comma follows the verb.

> Kimiko said, "I want to be a forensic scientist."

If the speaker comes after the quotation, and there is no question mark or exclamation point, a comma is used before the quotation mark.

> "This backpack is heavy," complained Jeff.
> Elena asked, "Why are you wearing it?"
> "I'm getting ready for the big hike this weekend," Jeff answered.

Unit 3 Using Language

© The Continental Press, Inc.   Do not duplicate.

Place quotation marks and commas where they belong in these sentences.

1. You have to admire a man like Korczak Ziolkowski Erin said.

2. She explained He spent the last 35 years of his life carving a statue out of a mountain.

3. What does the statue show? asked Tamar.

4. It is of Chief Crazy Horse, who was a hero of the Sioux people said Erin.

5. The statue is 563 feet high and 600 feet long she added.

6. That's gigantic! exclaimed Tamar.

- Quotation marks are also used before and after the titles of short works such as stories, poems, magazine articles, chapters in a book, songs, or TV shows.

STORY:	"The Necklace"
POEM:	"Chicago"
ARTICLE:	"The Rising Price of Gas"
CHAPTER:	"After the Vietnam War"
SONG:	"America the Beautiful"
TV SHOW:	"Endless Adventure"

- The titles of longer works such as books, magazines, movies, and plays are underlined.

BOOK:	Debt of Honor
MAGAZINE:	Road and Track
MOVIE:	The Runaway Jury
PLAY:	Hairspray

Use the correct punctuation for the titles in each sentence below.

1. A Study in Scarlet was the book that introduced Sherlock Holmes to the world.

2. One of the most important chapters in the self-help book is Being Your Own Best Friend.

3. Movies were silent until The Jazz Singer was made in 1927.

4. Lorraine Hansberry based her first play, A Raisin in the Sun, on her own life in Chicago.

5. Did you watch Sesame Street when you were a child?

6. The Celebrated Jumping Frog of Calaveras County was one of Mark Twain's earliest stories.

© The Continental Press, Inc.   Do not duplicate.

The Comma

- **Commas** have many uses. They often indicate a pause. For example, a comma is used to separate the name of a person being spoken to from the rest of a sentence.

   Jessie, are you going home now?
   I'll be leaving in a minute, Ben.

- A comma is used to separate the day from the year in a date.

   May 30, 1946   May 1, 2006

- A comma is used to separate the year in a date from the rest of a sentence.

   On November 11, 1918, World War I ended.

   Add commas where they are needed in the sentences below.

   1. Sharelle my cousin is coming to town!

   2. Why are you so excited Ramón?

   3. I haven't seen him since January 3 1999.

   4. On March 7 1999 he went into the army.

   5. And ever since Sharelle he has been travelling all around the world.

   6. I hope I get to meet him Ramón.

- A comma is used to separate the name of a city from the name of a state.

   Denver, Colorado   Richmond, Virginia

- A comma is also used to separate the name of the state from the rest of a sentence.

   Chicago, Illinois, was once just a trading post.

   Add commas where they are needed in the sentences below.

   1. This book about Nashville Tennessee tells a lot about country music.

   2. Many country albums are made in Los Angeles California too.

   3. There is a great jazz club in Portland Oregon where we went on vacation.

   4. We drove from San Antonio Texas to Norman Oklahoma on route 35.

- A comma is used to separate an appositive from the rest of a sentence. An appositive is a group of words that explain another word. Two commas are needed to set off the appositive unless it comes at the beginning or end of the sentence.

   Mother Teresa, the woman who won the 1979 Nobel Peace Prize, lived in India.
   The 1979 Nobel Peace Prize went to Mother Teresa, a woman who lived in India.

© The Continental Press, Inc.   Do not duplicate.

Add commas where they belong in the sentences below.

1. Not long ago, it wasn't safe to swim in Lake Erie the farthest south of the Great Lakes because of pollution.

2. Katrina a hurricane caused a lot of damage to the Gulf Coast.

3. People sometimes dial 911 the number to report emergencies when they really don't need to.

4. Tornadoes fierce and twisting wind storms can travel up to 40 miles an hour.

- A comma is used to separate items in a series. Sometimes these items are single words.

  The United States flag is red, white, and blue.

Sometimes the items in a series are groups of words or phrases. A comma still follows each item before the word *and.*

  Ginger smacked the ball, dashed for first base, and slid in safely.

Sometimes adjectives are used in a series. A comma is used to separate them if the word *and* is missing.

  a hot, stuffy, sticky day
  soft, fluffy pillows

Add commas where they are needed in the sentences below.

1. You can't hurt yourself if you fall in one of those new soft light bathtubs.

2. Charlie Chaplin Harold Lloyd and Buster Keaton were famous comics in silent movies.

3. At a health fair, people can have their eyes examined have their hearts checked and get many tests done—all for free.

4. Most dinosaurs were probably not huge fierce meat-eating creatures.

5. The four planets closest to the sun are Mercury Venus Earth and Mars.

6. None of us wanted to enter the old dark damp cellar.

- A comma is used after words that introduce a sentence or connect the sentence back to the one that came before. Sometimes these are single words like *yes, no, well, indeed, however,* and *therefore.*

  Yes, I'd like to see the football game.
  However, I may have to work on Saturday.

Sometimes the introductory words are phrases such as *in fact, in other words, of course, needless to say,* and so on. A comma follows the introductory phrase.

  Needless to say, I hope I win the contest.

© The Continental Press, Inc.　Do not duplicate.

Words and phrases such as *however* and *in fact* can also appear within a sentence. Since they are not really necessary to understand the meaning of a sentence, they are called parenthetical expressions. A comma is used before and after a parenthetical expression to separate it from the rest of the sentence.

> Poison ivy, to be sure, is a plant to stay away from.

- A comma is usually used to separate a participial phrase from the rest of a sentence. A participle is a verb form used as an adjective to modify a noun. Participles usually end in *-ing* or *-ed*. They can be used alone or in a phrase with other words that modify or explain it.

> Panting, Lisa ran to make her train.
> The tired teacher, gasping for air, sank into her seat for the long ride home.
> Seated at last, Lisa pulled out her book.

Add commas where they are needed in the sentences below.

1. Our fierce guard dog sleeping soundly never even heard the thief.

2. Cell phones as a matter of fact are becoming more and more important in our lives.

3. Well look who's here!

4. Added and subtracted correctly your checking account should balance.

5. Carrying both bags of groceries Val almost tripped going up the stairs.

- A comma is used before the conjunction, or connecting word, in a compound sentence. A compound sentence has two independent clauses, clauses that can stand alone. The conjunctions that usually join these clauses in a compound sentence are *and, or,* and *but*.

> Teresa is a champion swimmer, and her brother is also very good.
> They spend hours practicing at the pool, or they go over to the lake.
> They don't have time for much else, but that doesn't seem to bother them.

- A comma is also used in some complex sentences. A complex sentence has an independent clause that can stand alone and at least one dependent clause that does not make sense without the rest of the sentence. Many dependent clauses begin with words such as *since, when, although, because, until, after, before, unless,* and *while*. If this kind of dependent clause comes first in a sentence, a comma is used after it.

> When the telephone rang, Jerry jumped up.

- Another kind of dependent clause begins with a word such as *who, which,* or *that* and modifies, or tells about, a noun. If that noun is already clearly identified in the sentence, commas are used to separate the clause from the rest of the sentence.

> Amelia Earhart, who was a famous flier, disappeared on July 2, 1937.

© The Continental Press, Inc.   Do not duplicate.

Add commas where they are needed in the sentences below.

1. Some fish live in salt water but they will travel long distances to lay their eggs in fresh water.

2. After I added sugar to the lemonade it tasted too sweet.

3. Scott Turow who writes thrilling mysteries was a lawyer before becoming a writer.

4. Although Ruben had the best record another player won the award.

5. One of the oldest cities in the United States is St. Augustine which is in Florida.

6. Jason started laughing and he almost couldn't stop.

The Apostrophe

An **apostrophe** is used to show ownership or a close relationship.

- After a singular noun, the apostrophe is followed by *s*.

                Amy's report   the dentist's office

- If a noun is plural and already ends in *s*, an apostrophe comes after the *s*.

            the workers' problems   parents' duties

- If a plural noun does not end in *s*, add an apostrophe and *s* to show ownership.

             men's haircuts   the children's store

Add an apostrophe or an apostrophe and *s* to make the underlined word in each sentence below show ownership.

1. The <u>robin</u>   nest had fallen from the tree.

2. The <u>tourists</u>   car wouldn't start.

3. <u>Hideo</u>   answer was correct.

4. My <u>friend</u>   brother is a freshman.

5. <u>Children</u>   shoes should fit comfortably.

6. The <u>men</u>   department is on the third floor.

7. The <u>Johnsons</u>   house burned down.

8. The <u>women</u>   jobs were difficult.

- An apostrophe is also used in a contraction. A contraction is made up of two words written together with one or more letters left out. The apostrophe takes the place of the missing letters.

          could not   →   couldn∅t   →   couldn't
          I have   →   I h∕ave   →   I've

© The Continental Press, Inc.   Do not duplicate.

Write the contraction that is made by joining each pair of words below.

1. have not _____
2. I am _____
3. they are _____
4. was not _____

5. let us _____
6. she will _____
7. has not _____
8. we are _____

SPELLING

Correct spelling is an important part of writing well. The English language, however, can be confusing.

The spelling of a word may change if an ending is added, as in *drop* and *dropped* or *happy* and *happiest.*

The same sound may be spelled differently, as in *ate* and *break* or *note* and *crow.*

And the same spelling may have different sounds, as in *rough, though,* and *through.*

Even people who have studied English for many years may not be sure about how to spell a word. But you can make your spelling better with practice. Here are some tips to help you become a better speller.

- *Use a dictionary.* Sooner or later, almost everyone needs a dictionary to check spelling. If you are not sure about the correct spelling of a word, look it up. You'll end up with fewer spelling errors.

- *Keep a list of words you have misspelled.* Every person has problems with different words. Whenever you misspell a word, add the correct spelling to your list of problem words. Underline the letters that give you trouble. Look at your list often. That way you'll learn the correct spelling of those words.

- *Learn the basic patterns of spelling.* Words are formed in certain ways. There are often exceptions, or words that don't fit the usual patterns. But learning the basic spelling patterns will still be very helpful to you.

Homophones

Homophones are words that sound alike but are spelled differently and have different meanings. These word pairs, for example, are homophones.

rode—road   weigh—way   scent—cent

Some homophones are particular problems because we use them so much.

- *Two* means "the number 2."

    Giselle ordered two hamburgers.

- *Too* means "also" or "more than enough."

    She asked for a soda, too.   The food took too long.

© The Continental Press, Inc.   Do not duplicate.

- *To* means "toward" or is used with verbs.

  > Giselle left and walked to the corner to catch her bus.

- *Its* means "belonging to it."

  > A snake sheds its skin.

- *It's* is the contraction for "it is."

  > It's raining.

- *Here* means "in this place" or is used to begin a sentence before a linking verb, such as *is*, *are*, *was*, or *were*.

  > Pat stacked the wood here by the fireplace.
  > Here are the matches, too.

- *Hear* means "to listen."

  > Even in the back row, we could hear the speaker.

- *There* means "in that place" or is used to begin a sentence before a linking verb, such as *is*, *are*, *was*, or *were*.

  > Let's sit over there.
  > There are enough chairs for everyone.

- *Their* means "belonging to them."

  > Some trees lose their leaves in the fall.

- *They're* is the contraction for "they are."

  > The workers say that they're not paid enough.

- *Your* means "belonging to you."

  > Why isn't your name on the list?

- *You're* is the contraction for "you are."

  > You're next to see the doctor.

- *Whose* means "belonging to whom."

  > Whose keys are these?

- *Who's* is the contraction for "who is."

  > Who's asking?

© The Continental Press, Inc.   Do not duplicate.

Underline the correct homophone to complete the sentences below.

1. Old Tiger can't (hear/here) very well anymore.

2. Always lock (your/you're) car when you leave it.

3. Male and female geese pair up, and the (too/two) of them stay together for life.

4. The snowplow cleared the snow off the street, but (its/it's) piled up against the parked cars.

5. (Whose/Who's) invited to the party?

6. Our cats seem to think that (their/they're) people.

7. If (your/you're) not careful with a paperback book, (its/it's) pages will fall out.

8. The players really like (there/their) new coach.

9. Chocolate is my favorite ice cream, but I like strawberry, (too/to).

10. We have (two/to) wait (here/hear) for the nurse.

Suffixes

- A **suffix** is a letter or group of letters added to the end of a word. Some suffixes are used to change the form of words. Endings are used to make singular nouns plural (*tiger* + *s* = *tigers*). They are used to make -*s* form and past tense verbs (*reach* + *es* = *reaches*, *ask* + *ed* = *asked*). They are also used to make the comparing forms of adjectives and adverbs (*tall* + *est* = *tallest*, *soon* + *er* = *sooner*). Knowing how to add the endings will help you spell all these forms correctly.

The spelling of most words stays the same when a suffix is added.

hero + es = heroes   laugh + ed = laughed
run + s = runs   rich + er = richer
fast + est = fastest

Spell the word made by adding the given suffix to each word below.

1. add + ed = _____

2. toss + es = _____

3. soon + er = _____

4. dish + es = _____

5. deep + est = _____

6. airplane + s = _____

7. know + s = _____

8. lunch + es = _____

9. high + er = _____

10. rich + est = _____

- If a word ends in a **consonant plus** *y*, the *y* is usually changed to *i* before a suffix is added.

country + es = countries   funny + er = funnier
hurry + ed = hurried   easy + est = easiest

© The Continental Press, Inc.   Do not duplicate.

Remember, however, that if a word ends in a **vowel plus** *y,* usually no change is made.

key + s = keys   enjoy + ed = enjoyed

- If a word ends in *e,* the *e* is usually dropped when a suffix beginning with a vowel is added.

live + ed = lived   brave + er = braver

However, the *e* is usually kept if the suffix is, or begins with, a consonant.

hike + s = hikes   dance + s = dances

- Sometimes the final consonant of a word is doubled when a suffix beginning with a vowel is added. This happens if the word has one syllable and ends in a consonant-vowel-consonant pattern.

stop + ed = stopped   rub + ing = rubbing
thin + er = thinner   hot + est = hottest

It also occurs with words of more than one syllable if the last syllable is stressed (spoken loudest) and ends in a consonant-vowel-consonant.

begin + ing = beginning

However, if the final consonant is *w, x,* or *y,* no change is made.

new + est = newest   mix + ing = mixing   play + ed = played

Spell the word made by adding the given suffix to each word below.

1. fence + s =   _____

2. penny + es =   _____

3. believe + ed =   _____

4. bounce + ing = _____

5. cozy + est =   _____

6. wide + er =   _____

7. hive + s =   _____

8. safe + est =   _____

9. monkey + s =   _____

10. stay + ed =   _____

Irregular Forms

- Not all words change form by adding suffixes. Some words have **irregular forms.** This means that they do not follow a pattern. Knowing how to spell the irregular forms can be a real problem. Always use a dictionary if you are not sure how to spell a form of a word. Irregular plural forms, irregular past forms, and irregular comparing forms are often listed in the dictionary right after the entry word. They look something like this:

go\gō\ *v* **went**\went\; **gone**\gȯn\ **1:** move ahead **2:** leave

good\gȯd\ *adj* **better**\betʹər\; **best**\best\ **1:** of a favorable character **2:** right **3:** kind

goose\güs\ *n, pl* **geese**\gēs\ **1:** a large bird with a long neck **2:** a silly person

© The Continental Press, Inc.   Do not duplicate.

Write the plural form of each noun below. Use a dictionary if you need help.

1. child   _____

2. tooth   _____

3. mouse   _____

4. foot   _____

5. woman   _____

Spell the past form of each verb below. Use a dictionary if you need help.

1. do   _____

2. catch   _____

3. begin   _____

4. ride   _____

5. find   _____

Spell the comparative and superlative forms of each adjective or adverb below. Use a dictionary if you need help.

1. good   _____

2. little   _____

3. much   _____

4. well   _____

5. far   _____

Prefixes

• A letter or group of letters added to the beginning of a word is called a **prefix.** Words with prefixes are not hard to spell. Just remember never to add or drop any letters.

un + able = unable   dis + satisfied = dissatisfied

TROUBLESOME WORDS

• One of the hardest tasks in spelling is remembering when to write *ie* and when to write *ei*. If the sound of the letters is long *e*, as in piece, the *i* usually comes first.

achieve	belief	fiend	thief	field
believe	chief	niece	yield	piece

However, after the letter *c*, the *e* usually comes first.

ceiling	deceive	perceive	receive

© The Continental Press, Inc.   Do not duplicate.

The *e* also usually comes first if the letters have a sound other than long *e*.

eight	height	their	weigh
foreign	neighbor	vein	weight

Remember that there are some exceptions to these patterns.

fierce	friend	leisure	weird

Find the misspelled word in each sentence below. Cross it out and write the correct spelling in the margin.

1. The cheif spoke to the press about the strange case.

2. A blue whale may wiegh 150 tons.

3. This cieling needs a new coat of paint.

4. Terrell is one of my best freinds.

5. The feirce storm blew over quickly.

6. Our new nieghbors are interesting people.

- Some spelling problems occur when we confuse two words. Sound out each syllable of a word before you try to spell it. Also remember the meaning you have in mind when you spell a word.

Here are some word pairs that are often confused:

choose—means "to pick"
chose—is a past tense verb that means "picked"

desert—means "a very dry place"
dessert—means "the last course of a meal"

later—means "coming afterward" or "not as early"
latter—means "the last of a group being talked about"

sense—means "to be aware of" or "meaning"
since—means "from a certain time in the past" or "because"

than—is a word used in comparisons
then—means "next"

lead—means "to show the way" or "to be first"
led—is a past tense verb that means "showed the way" or "was first"

quiet—means "not noisy"
quite—means "completely" or "rather"
quit—means "to give up or stop"

© The Continental Press, Inc.   Do not duplicate.

Find the misspelled words in the sentences below. Cross out each one and write the correct spelling above it.

1. Sense it's Ben's birthday, he gets to chose the desert.

2. Does he like apple pie more then cake?

3. Both are quit good.

4. Ben's parents can led the singing.

5. Latter Ben will open his presents.

Some words seem to give everyone more trouble than others. Remind yourself to look them up when you use them and learn how to spell them correctly.

Here is a list of some words that are often misspelled. Notice that the list includes a number of homophones, which are entered together. The list ends on page 143.

a lot (allot)	boundary	curious
abundance	brake (break)	cylinder
accept	breadth	dangerously
accommodate	breath	daughter
account	breathe	deceive
ache	bureau	definite
acquaint	business	decent
acquire	calendar	descend
advertise	campaign	descent (dissent)
advice	capital (capitol)	despair
advise	careless	discipline
affect	carriage	doubt
aisle (isle)	ceiling (sealing)	eighth
all ready (already)	choose	either
all right	chose	endeavor
analysis	cite (sight, site)	enough
analyze	clot	ether
angel	clothes	exaggerate
angle	coarse (course)	except
argue	column	exercise
arguing	committee	exhaust
assistance	competition	familiar
ate (eight)	complement	fascinate
autumn	(compliment)	fatigue
bargain	conceal	February
beginning	conceit	foreign
believe	conscience	forty
belief	conscious	freight
benefit	convenience	gardener
benefited	convenient	governor
board (bored)	courtesy	grammar

© The Continental Press, Inc.　Do not duplicate.

grateful
guarantee
guard
guidance
guide
handkerchief
heard (herd)
height
hole (whole)
humor
humorous
imitate
imagine
imaginary
immediate
independence
independent
innocence
innocent
interest
interrupt
island
its (it's)
jealous
journal
judgment
judicious
kindly
kindergarten
kitchen
knew (new)
know (no)
knowledge
laboratory
laugh
leisure
library
license
loose
lose
maintenance
marriage
marry
merry
medicine
miniature

mischief
mischievous
misspell
mortgage
muscle
muscular
mystery
naive
necessary
neighbor
neither
niece
obstacle
occasion
occasionally
occur
occurrence
omission
omit
once
ounce
pair (pare, pear)
parallel
parent
pastime
peace (piece)
permanent
persistence
persistent
personal
personnel
persuade
peruse
plain (plane)
pleasant
pleasure
possession
potato
precede
prescription
principal (principle)
probably
proceed
profession
profit (prophet)
psychology

psychosis
pursue
rain (reign)
raise (raze)
receipt
recipe
recommend
recommendation
rehearse
repeat
repetition
resemble
resemblance
resist
restaurant
rhyme
rhythm
sandwich
scene (seen)
schedule
scissors
seize
separate
sergeant
severe
siege
significance
significant
stationary (stationery)
straight (strait)
succeed
suit
suite (sweet)
superintendent
surprise
sweat
syllable
symmetrical
symmetry
sympathy
sympathetic
synonym
temperament
temperature
temporary
temporarily

Unit 3 Using Language

© The Continental Press, Inc.   Do not duplicate.

tendency	treasury	villain
their (there, they're)	tries	wait (weight)
therefore	truly	way (weigh)
thorough	unnecessary	weather (whether)
though	unusual	weak (week)
threw (through)	useful	which
tomorrow	vain (vane, vein)	witch
tongue	variety	while
tragedy	vicious	whose (who's)
tragic	view	your (you're)
treasurer	village	zealous

In the sentences below, underline the correctly spelled word in parentheses.

1. This is a (pleasent/pleasant) (occasion/ocasion).

2. We (deskused/discussed) the fact that I like only one (character/caracter) in the (entire/intire) play.

3. Small, sharp (sisors/scissors) are (excellent/exallent) for cutting hair.

4. Police (immediately/imediatley) answered my call.

5. There are (fiscal/physical) (differences/diferrances) between a cheetah and a leopard.

6. The old bull was kept in a (seperate/separate) pen.

7. That movie will (dissapoint/disappoint) you.

© The Continental Press, Inc.   Do not duplicate.

Lesson 4

Editing and Proofreading

After you finish writing, there is still work to be done. You will need to edit and proofread your work. Proofreading means reviewing your writing for mistakes. Editing means correcting those mistakes and making other changes to improve your writing.

Editing

To edit is to improve your writing by:

- organizing the ideas

- refining the style

- correcting mistakes in grammar and sentence structure

When you edit, you are correcting mistakes in your draft. Editing is also a way to improve the organization and style of your writing. You can improve the organization by moving sentences or by adding, removing, and rewriting sentences. You can improve the style by making sure that the structure of the sentences is varied in length and type. You can also improve the style by substituting more precise or vivid words for words that are not very descriptive.

3.3.1 The student will edit texts for spelling, capitalization, and punctuation.

3.3.2 The student will use available resources to correct or confirm revisions and/or editorial choices.

Proofreading

Proofreading means checking the grammar, spelling, punctuation, and capitalization in your writing. When you are proofreading for grammatical errors, it is a good idea to read your work aloud. Sometimes it is easier to catch mistakes in grammar when you hear them.

Mistakes in punctuation, spelling, and capitalization are easier to see. Use a dictionary to help you spell words correctly. Use a style handbook as a reference for questions about punctuation and capitalization.

Sometimes it is difficult to proofread your own work. You might not see your own errors. It is helpful to ask someone else to proofread your work. This will show you the kinds of mistakes you tend to make and help you avoid making the same mistakes in the future.

© The Continental Press, Inc.   Do not duplicate.

Guided Practice

These paragraphs are part of a draft about sharks and remoras. Read the paragraphs. Then answer the questions.

---

¹The shark is known as the king of the sea. ²It is probably the most feared animal of the ocean. ³Not all fish are afraid of <u>sharks though</u>. ⁴The remora is a fish that seeks out the company of sharks. ⁵Remoras are much smaller than sharks, and they have no way to protect <u>themself</u> from a shark's snapping jaws.

⁶The remora is protected by the symbiotic nature of its relationship with the shark. ⁷This means that remoras and sharks help each other. ⁸The remora hitches a ride on a shark by attaching itself to the shark with a fin. ⁹Remoras share in the shark's meals. ¹⁰In return, the remora cleans parasites off the shark's skin.

Which of these sentences <u>best</u> combines the ideas in Sentences 1 and 2 into one sentence?

A The shark is known as the king of the sea, it is probably the most feared animal of the ocean.

B Known as the king of the sea, the shark is probably the most feared animal of the ocean.

C The shark is known as the king of the sea and it is probably the most feared animal of the ocean.

D The known king of the sea, the shark probably the most feared animal of the ocean.

When you look at the answer choices, you can eliminate A, which is a run-on sentence. Choice D can be eliminated when you realize that it does not have a predicate (verb) to show the main action of the sentence. Choice C is a complete sentence, but it lacks a comma and is dull. Choice B is the best answer.

Which of these is the correct way to edit the underlined part of Sentence 3?

F sharks, though   H sharks; though

G sharks: though   J Best as it is

This question has to do with punctuation. You know that a colon is used to introduce a list, so choice G does not fit. A semi-colon is used to separate two complete sentences, which means choice H can be eliminated. The sentence does need some punctuation, though. Choice F is the best answer.

© The Continental Press, Inc.   Do not duplicate.

Which of these is the correct way to edit the underlined part of Sentence 5?

    A theirselves

    B oneself

    C itself

    D themselves

Remember that pronouns are used in place of nouns. This means they must agree with the nouns they replace. If the noun is plural, such as "remoras," the pronoun used to refer to the noun must be plural, too. This means you can eliminate choices B and C. Choice A can be eliminated because it is not a correct way to write the pronoun. Choice D is the best answer.

Which of these sentences would best follow Sentence 5?

    F What keeps these fish from becoming the catch of the day?

    G Remoras help the sharks and the sharks help the remoras.

    H A shark gives the remora a place to rest.

    J How could such a small fish help a shark?

This question is about the organization of the draft. The sentence that will fit after Sentence 5 will be one that provides a transition from the ideas in the first paragraph to the ideas in the second. Look at all the answer choices. The only one that links the ideas in both paragraphs is choice F.

These paragraphs are part of a draft about basketball. Read the paragraphs. Then answer the questions.

¹Basketball is an international sport that is played in nearly every country in the world. ²Americans invented the game, and they are still some of the world's best players. ³That's why you'll find American basketball players playing internationally. ⁴That is why American players can be found on pro rosters from Iceland to Australia. ⁵They can be found in the Middle East and in South America.

⁶Who are the Americans who play professional basketball abroad? ⁷Most are former college players who do not quite have the skill or stamina needed to play in the <u>american national basketball association.</u> ⁸Still love basketball, though, and welcome the opportunity to get paid for playing the game they love. ⁹Most find it easy to adapt to the rules in their host country, as there are differences in how the game is played from country to country.

© The Continental Press, Inc.   Do not duplicate.

Which of these transitional expressions is <u>best</u> to use at the beginning of Sentence 2?

    A Moreover,   **C** In other words,

    B However,   **D** In addition,

This question is about how the ideas in the draft are linked from sentence to sentence. When you look at Sentences 1 and 2, you can see that Sentence 2 gives information in contrast to the information in Sentence 1. Choice B is the only answer choice that has a transitional expression indicating contrast.

Which of these sentences should be removed from the draft to avoid repeating ideas?

    F Sentence 1   **H** Sentence 6

    G Sentence 3   **J** Sentence 9

This question is about the organization of the draft. Look at Sentences 1, 3, 6, and 9. The only sentence that repeats ideas in another sentence is choice G, Sentence 3.

Which of these is the correct way to edit the underlined part of Sentence 7?

    A American National Basketball Association

    B American national basketball association

    C American National basketball association

    D Best as it is

The word "American" is a proper noun, even when it is used to modify another noun, as it is in this sentence, so it must be capitalized. The National Basketball Association is the name of an official organization and is also a proper noun. Choice A is the best answer.

Which is the <u>best</u> way to write Sentence 8?

    F They still love basketball, though, and welcome the opportunity to get paid for playing the game they love.

    G Still love basketball, and welcome the opportunity to get paid for playing the game they love.

    H They still love basketball, welcome the opportunity to get paid for playing the game they love.

    J Still loving basketball, though, and welcome the opportunity to get paid for playing the game they love.

The error in Sentence 8 is that it is missing a subject. Choices G and J do not correct this error, so they can be eliminated. Choice H adds a subject, but also adds a new error by removing the word *and*. Choice F is the best answer.

© The Continental Press, Inc.   Do not duplicate.

Test Yourself

These paragraphs are part of a draft about the North Pole. Read the paragraphs. Then answer Numbers 1 through 4.

> ¹There are not many lands in the world that do not belong to a country. ²However, the North Pole is one area of land that does not come under the jurisdiction of a particular country. ³It is considered neutral territory. ⁴This is not the only reason the North Pole is unusual. ⁵It is one of only two places on the surface of the Earth that get six months of daylight. ⁶Until the next six months, the North Pole is in complete darkness and receives no light from the sun.
>
> ⁷You might think that the warmth from the sunlight would melt the ice that covers the North Pole, but the North Pole is too far from the sun. ⁸Whether it is light or dark the North Pole is usually covered in ice.

1 Which of these sentences <u>best</u> combines the ideas in Sentences 2 and 3 into one sentence?

  A However, the North Pole is one area of land that does not come under the jurisdiction of a particular country, it is considered neutral territory.

  B However, the North Pole is one area of land that does not come under the jurisdiction of a particular country, is considered neutral territory.

  C However, the North Pole is one area of land that does not come under the jurisdiction of a particular country it is considered neutral territory.

  D However, the North Pole is one area of land that does not come under the jurisdiction of a particular country and is considered neutral territory.

2 Which of these prepositions <u>best</u> replaces the underlined word in Sentence 6?

  F During   **H** Between

  G After   **J** Among

3 Read this sentence.

> Recently, however, people have observed water at the North Pole.

Which is the <u>best</u> place for this sentence?

  A before Sentence 1   **C** between Sentences 5 and 6

  B between Sentences 3 and 4   **D** following Sentence 8

© The Continental Press, Inc.   Do not duplicate.

4 Which of these is the correct way to edit the underlined part of Sentence 8?

    F dark. The

    G dark, the

    H dark: The

    J dark; the

These paragraphs are part of a draft about scientific theories. Read the paragraphs. Then answer Numbers 5 through 9.

> ¹Science never stands still. ²Science and our understanding of life and the universe is ever changing. ³New ideas are <u>proposed debated, and sometimes</u> ridiculed. ⁴Many theories that are now widely accepted were once laughed at.
>
> ⁵Consider one well-known scientific <u>question; What</u> wiped out the dinosaurs? ⁶Most people know that a giant asteroid crashed into Earth about 65 million years ago. ⁷The impact of the crash kicked up dust and dirt that blocked the sun. ⁸Blocking the sun disrupted the food chain.
>
> ⁹This does not completely answer the question about dinosaur extinction. ¹⁰However, most scientists agree that the asteroid theory is likely to be true. ¹¹This is the modern explanation for the mass extinctions on Earth. ¹²It is interesting to note that when Luis and Walter Alvarez first proposed this theory, many scientists thought it was <u>stupid</u>.

5 Which of these is the correct way to edit the underlined part of Sentence 3?

    A proposed: debated and sometimes

    B proposed, debated, and sometimes

    C proposed debated; and sometimes

    D proposed. Debated, and sometimes

6 Which of these is the correct way to edit the underlined part of Sentence 5?

    F question, what

    G question. What

    H question What

    J question: What

© The Continental Press, Inc.   Do not duplicate.

7 Which of these sentences <u>best</u> combines the ideas in Sentences 7 and 8 into one sentence?

  A The impact of the crash kicked up dust and dirt that blocked the sun, which disrupted the food chain.

  B Blocking the sun, the impact of the crash kicked up dust and dirt and disrupted the food chain.

  C Disrupting the food chain, the impact of the crash kicked up dust and dirt, blocking the sun.

  D The impact of the crash kicked up dust and dirt, blocking the sun, disrupting the food chain.

8 Which word <u>best</u> replaces the underlined word in Sentence 12?

  F crazy

  G dumb

  H ridiculous

  J idiotic

9 Which of these sentences should be removed from the draft to avoid repeating ideas?

  A Sentence 1

  B Sentence 3

  C Sentence 4

  D Sentence 6

© The Continental Press, Inc.   Do not duplicate.

UNIT 4

EVALUATING TEXT

Even though you may not be aware of the process that goes on in your mind, you often evaluate or make judgments about what you read. For example, you might read a newspaper headline or the first paragraph of an article and decide to stop reading because the topic seems boring or uninteresting to you. Or you might read a story and think that it sounds so far-fetched that it can't be true. Much of the reading you do, including reading for school assignments and tests, requires you to first analyze (or figure out) some things about the text and then evaluate (make judgments about) what you read.

The goal of this unit is that you will be able to demonstrate the ability to evaluate the content, organization, and language use of the texts or written materials that you read.

Lesson 1

Analyzing Text

When you read a story, novel, or passage on a test, you are usually affected in some way. The passage might make you reflect on experiences in your own life, give you insight into human nature, or cause you to feel different emotions. Analyzing text requires you to think about and describe the effect that a passage has on you as the reader.

4.1.1 The student will state and explain a personal response to a given text.

4.2.4 The student will explain how repetitions of words, phrases, structural features, and ideas affect the meaning and/or tone of a text.

One way an author achieves certain effects is by using repetition. Repeating words, phrases, or even organizational features within a passage will affect the meaning or the tone of a passage, which then has an effect on the reader.

© The Continental Press, Inc.   Do not duplicate.

Guided Practice

Reread the story excerpt on page 109. Then answer the question.

The effect of the repetition of the words "These stories" in the last two sentences of the excerpt is to

    A amuse the reader

    B hypnotize the reader

    C make the stories sound more interesting

    D emphasize the significance of the stories

> Think about the effect of the repetition. It does not amuse you or hypnotize you. Nor does it make the stories sound more interesting. The effect is to make the stories seem even more significant. Choice D is the best answer.

Reread the poem "The Sky Is Low, the Clouds Are Mean" on page 16.

Here is an example of an open-ended question (BCR) that asks you to analyze the structure of the poem:

> **The poem alternates long and short lines. Write an explanation that describes the effect the structure of the poem has on you as the reader. Support your explanation with details and examples from the poem.**

Here is an example of an open-ended question (ECR) that asks you to analyze the effects of the poem on the reader:

> **Write an essay that describes how the poem affects you as the reader. Support your explanation with details and examples from the poem.**

Reread the poem "Sammy Sosa Comes Home" on page 46, and answer the question.

Which word describes the effect the poem <u>most likely</u> has on the reader?

    F inspiring   **H** refreshing

    G amusing   **J** frightening

> Think about the effect of the poem. There is nothing especially humorous or frightening in the poem, so you can eliminate choices G and J. Choice H, refreshing, does not make sense for this poem. Choice F is the best answer.

© The Continental Press, Inc.   Do not duplicate.

Now read this article and answer the questions that follow.

Computers on the Job

Since you were young, you have probably asked yourself "What will I do when I'm finished with school?" You probably still don't know. Whatever you decide to do, you will probably be required to use a computer. Computers will make your job easier because they will do part of the work.

Information Please

catalog: *n. a list of items in a collection, usually with descriptions*

We searched several *catalogs* for the best prices on bicycle tires.

Computers can store a great deal of information. Then they make it easy for you to find the information. Think about the library. Some libraries still have card **catalogs,** but many use computers. Card catalogs store the names of books and authors on cards. They include at least three cards for every book. Most libraries have only one card catalog. If you want to find a book about llamas and someone else is using the "L" drawer, you have to wait. In a library with a computer, you can search for books at the same time other people are looking.

Often the librarian can help you find books at other libraries that you can use, too. The computer stores information about all the libraries in a system. And the library computer keeps track of who takes out a book and when it is returned. Everyone in the library—even readers—uses a computer.

What's Wrong?

diagnose: *v. to identify a medical illness or a problem*

Doctors examine patients and use tests to *diagnose* an illness.

Computers can help **diagnose** problems. What happens when a car breaks down? Chances are that a computer will be used to find out what is wrong. Computers inside cars send drivers information when something is going wrong. And computers can help the mechanic fix a problem by showing where the problem is. Car designers use computers, too. The computers help them create a picture of what a new car will look like. They can work out many problems before the car is even built.

Computers help diagnose medical problems, too. If you have tests in a hospital or doctor's office, a computer will probably analyze those tests. The computer can help the doctors decide what is wrong and how serious the problem is.

Computers can even diagnose their own problems! They warn users when something is going wrong. Sometimes a computer will tell you to shut it off while it works on the problem.

Unit 4 Evaluating Text

153

© The Continental Press, Inc.   Do not duplicate.

Count Me In

The word *compute* means "count." The first computers were designed to count and do other kinds of mathematics. So, of course, banks use computers. The bank's computers keep track of where every customer's money is. They have other functions, too. They use information to figure out who can borrow money. They compute the interest someone must pay to borrow money. And they share information with other banks. Everyone who works in a bank uses a computer.

Customers use the bank's computer. An ATM, or "automatic teller machine" is a computer. ATMs are often located outside a bank or in a store. Customers put in information, and the computer checks the information with the bank. Then the customer can take out money.

Even Uncle Sam Uses a Computer

The cash register at the supermarket is a computer. Stores can change prices or add discounts with a computer program.

Yes, even Uncle Sam has to know how to operate a computer! The United States government has been using computers for more than half a century. Today computers help the government do all of its work. Mail service is a good example. Although many people use e-mail to send messages, the U.S. Postal Service still handles millions of pieces of mail every day. Computers help the post office collect, sort, and deliver the mail quickly. Computers can read special codes printed on envelopes. They store important information about mail service. Postal service workers have to use computers every day.

See if you can figure out how a computer is used in each of these places: the school office, your favorite fast-food restaurant, a movie theater, a toll booth on the highway, a basketball game.

How would you use a computer if you worked in one of those places?

The **most likely** effect of the question in the first paragraph of the article is to

A   interest the reader

B   challenge the reader

C   obtain personal information from the reader

D   encourage the reader to pursue a career in computers

The question is obviously not asking for information, nor is it particularly encouraging the reader to pursue a career in computers. When you compare choices A and B, you can tell that choice B is the best answer.

© The Continental Press, Inc.   Do not duplicate.

Which feature of the article helps the reader find specific information in the article?

    F   the title

    G   the headings

    H   the words in bold print

    J   the definitions in the boxes

Think about the different features in the answer choices and how each feature helps the reader. The title tells the main idea of the article. The words in bold print highlight words that may be unfamiliar. The definitions in the boxes tell what the unfamiliar words mean. The headings are the only feature that help the reader find specific information. Choice G is the best answer.

BCR

Write an explanation that describes the effects of the article on you as a reader. Support your explanation with details and examples from the article.

What did you learn about computers on the job from this article? How does this knowledge affect you as you think about your future job? Make some notes about how computers are used and how this knowledge affects your thoughts and feelings. Then write a short response of one or two paragraphs on a separate sheet of paper.

Test Yourself

Read "The Gettysburg Address," a speech delivered by President Lincoln on November 19, 1863. Then answer Numbers 1 and 2.

The Gettysburg Address

Fourscore and seven years ago our fathers brought forth on this continent a new nation, conceived in liberty, and dedicated to the proposition that all men are created equal.

Now we are engaged in a great civil war, testing whether that nation or any nation, so conceived and so dedicated, can long endure. We are met on a great battlefield of that war. We have come to dedicate a portion of that field as a final resting-place for those who here gave their lives that this nation might live. It is altogether fitting and proper that we should do this.

But, in a larger sense, we cannot dedicate…we cannot consecrate…we cannot hallow…this ground. The brave men, living and dead, who struggled here, have consecrated it far above our poor power to add

© The Continental Press, Inc.   Do not duplicate.

or detract. The world will little note nor long remember what we say here, but it can never forget what they did here. It is for us the living rather to be dedicated here to the unfinished work which they who fought here have thus far so nobly advanced. It is rather for us to be here dedicated to the great task remaining before us—that from these honored dead we take increased devotion to that cause for which they gave the last full measure of devotion; that we here highly resolve that these dead shall not have died in vain; that this nation, under God, shall have a new birth of freedom, and that government of the people, by the people, for the people, shall not perish from the earth.

1 The <u>most likely</u> effect of Lincoln's speech was to convince people that

    A no one else should die in this war

    B words that are spoken are not very important

    C they should continue the struggle for freedom

    D nothing they could do could make up for the soldiers' sacrifice

 2 BCR Write an explanation that tells how the repetition of words and phrases in "The Gettysburg Address" affects the meaning and tone of the speech. Use details and examples from the text to support your explanation.

Use the space below to plan your response. Then write your final draft on a separate sheet of paper.

_____

_____

_____

_____

_____

_____

_____

_____

_____

156

Unit 4 Evaluating Text

© The Continental Press, Inc. Do not duplicate.

Reread "Song of the Freedmen" on page 54. Then answer Numbers 3 and 4.

3 Which of these features of the song best illustrates the idea that the soldiers are intent upon their purpose?

A   the image of slavery in the word "chains"

B   the biblical reference of "Pharaoh's land"

C   the rhyming of the words "soon" and "noon"

D   the repetition of the phrase "We are coming"

 4 BCR Write an explanation that tells how the song encouraged the African American soldiers who were fighting in the Civil War. Support your explanation with details and examples from the song.

Use the space below to plan your response. Then write your final draft on a separate sheet of paper.

_____

_____

_____

_____

_____

_____

_____

_____

_____

_____

_____

Reread the story "At the Fair" on pages 27–29. Then answer Numbers 5 through 8.

5 Which idea is repeated throughout the story?

A   Hard work is rewarding.

B   Nothing new ever happens.

C   Playing football takes discipline.

D   Nothing is the way that it seems.

Unit 4 Evaluating Text   **157**

© The Continental Press, Inc.   Do not duplicate.

6 Which of these features of Paragraph 2 <u>best</u> illustrates the tedium of the work in the dishwashing room?

    F the repetition of the word "same"

    G the onomatopoeia of the word "whoosh"

    H the hyperbole of the words "stacking up forever"

    J the alliteration of "same," "songs," and "summer"

7 Which word <u>best</u> describes the reader's feeling at the end of the story?

    A fear

    B hope

    C boredom

    D loneliness

 8 BCR There are many repeated words and phrases in the story. Write an explanation describing the effect of these repeated words and phrases on the reader. Support your explanation with details and examples from the story.

Use the space below to plan your response. Then write your final draft on a separate sheet of paper.

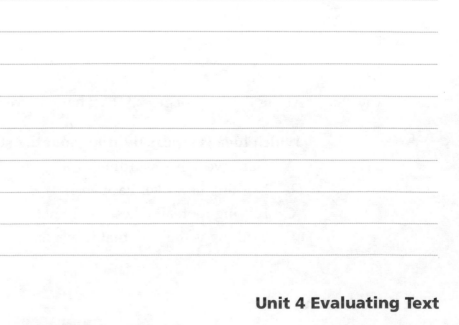

© The Continental Press, Inc.   Do not duplicate.

Lesson 2

Comparing and Contrasting Texts

When you read different texts on the same subject, you probably find yourself **comparing,** or looking for similarities, and **contrasting,** or looking for differences. You often do this naturally as your mind sorts and organizes the information you receive from reading.

If you are reading two literary passages, you may compare and contrast the style, tone, genre, or structure; or the narrative elements, such as the plot, characters, setting, conflict, or point of view.

While you could compare and contrast the style, tone, and structure of two informational passages, you might also examine the formatting (use of headings and other features of printed text), the author's attitude toward the subject, the use of supporting facts and details, and any other features that contribute to your understanding of the passages.

4.3.4 The student will compare the differences in effect of two texts on a given subject.

On a test, you can tell if you need to compare or contrast texts from the words used in the question.

Words that show comparison	Words that show contrast
alike	differ
both	different
common	difference
likeness	dissimilar
share	distinguish
similar	unlike
similarity	
same	

© The Continental Press, Inc.   Do not duplicate.

Guided Practice

Read the passages "Mobile Home of the Pioneers" and "Trail of Courage." Then answer the questions.

"Mobile Home" of the Pioneers

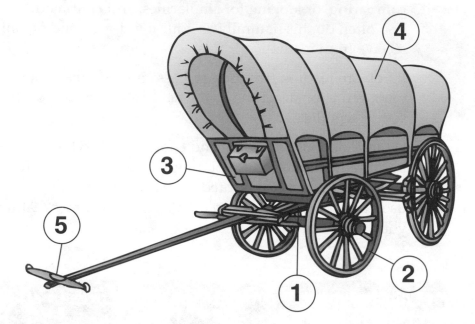

Covered wagons are famous in American history. As pioneers moved West, many traveled in a covered wagon called a "prairie schooner." A schooner is a kind of large ship. Some people thought that covered wagons looked like ships traveling on land instead of water. That's how they got the name.

1. The sturdy wooden base of the wagon was made from thick, heavy pieces of wood. The undercarriage had to be strong. The pioneer trails were almost always rough and bumpy.

2. The wheels were also made from wood. A flat iron "tire" fit over the rim. Nails connected the iron tire to the rim to protect the wood.

3. The wagon box held most of the pioneers' things. The box was about three feet deep. Cracks between the boards were filled with tar to protect the goods in the wagons from getting wet.

4. The best-known part of the prairie schooner was the cloth top. It was called the "bonnet." It was usually made of cotton material. The heavy cloth was sometimes painted with oil to help keep out the rain.

5. Most prairie schooners were pulled by mules or oxen. Mules could go faster, but oxen were cheaper. The oxen could also survive harsh weather better than mules. Still, pioneers often had to abandon their wagons in bad winter storms.

© The Continental Press, Inc.   Do not duplicate.

Trail of Courage

territory: *n. area of land*

territory: n. area of land

Before Oregon became a state in 1859, it was called the Oregon Territory.

It was early May in the year 1841. People were getting ready to leave Missouri. They were planning to make new homes in the western **territory**. They had a long, long way to travel in their sturdy prairie schooners. The trip would take about five months.

On a hill outside of Independence, Missouri, the first wagon train got ready. Toward the west there was plenty of wide-open land. There were few trees and no buildings or people. There were no roads. There wasn't even a trail!

The leader of the wagon train, John Bidwell, was a teacher and a farmer. He didn't know anything about the wilderness, and he didn't have a guide to show the way. Still, the settlers were ready to get started. It was hard to make a living in Missouri. They had heard there was good land in California and Oregon where they could have their own farms.

continent: n. a giant piece of land on the earth

Each *continent* on the earth has a name: Africa, Antarctica, Asia, Australia, Europe, North America, and South America.

Of course, Native Americans had lived in the west for thousands of years. A few European explorers and trappers had already crossed the **continent**. They had opened many different trails, but they didn't travel in heavy wagons loaded with supplies. And the European explorers and trappers rarely traveled with small children. No covered wagons had crossed the country before 1841.

Good Luck and Bad Luck

At first, the Bidwell wagon train had good luck. After just a few days on the trail, they met another group going west. This group had a guide, a mountain man whose name was Tom Fitzpatrick. For the first half of the journey, the two groups traveled together. They followed the Platte River across the flat land. There was plenty of water to drink and grass for the horses and oxen. The early days on the trail were easy.

Soon, however, the wagon train had to leave the river. The pioneers had to go north through the Rocky Mountains. Now it became harder to travel. Wagons sometimes broke down. Water and firewood material were harder to find. People and animals were tired. Because of Fitzpatrick's help, they made it halfway to the west.

At a place called Soda Springs, Fitzpatrick left to go in a different direction. Some of the Bidwell pioneers wanted to go on to Oregon. The rest wanted to keep on going to California. The two groups decided to split up. Now there was no one to guide and protect them. Still they went on.

© The Continental Press, Inc.　Do not duplicate.

Soon the weather began to change. Winter was coming. Supplies began running low. Some of the travelers got sick. Wagons broke down. One by one, the pioneers had to abandon their prairie schooners and continue on foot.

These pioneers were determined to survive. They would not quit. By the end of October, they had reached California and Oregon. They had very sore feet, but they had succeeded! Their success gave more pioneers the courage to move west.

If you travel to Oregon, you can learn more about the pioneers and wagon trains at the "End of the Trail" Museum in Oregon City.

During the next 24 years, thousands of people traveled on the pioneer trails. They all faced great hardships. But each year the trails grew easier to follow. Over time, the wagons wore tracks in the earth. In some places you can still see the tracks of the prairie schooners connecting the grassy plains. They remind us of the courage of the early western pioneers.

Which topic is addressed in both passages?

    A the way pioneers traveled

    B the length of the pioneers' trip

    C the number of pioneers that crossed the plains

    D the reason many pioneers chose to cross the plains

This question is about a subject that is addressed by both passages. You can eliminate choice B because the length of the trip is mentioned in "Trail of Courage," but not in the other passage. The same is true for choices C and D, as these topics are addressed only in "Trail of Courage." The only topic addressed in both passages is how the pioneers traveled, which means that choice A is the best answer.

Which detail appears in both passages?

    F Mules were faster, but oxen were cheaper.

    G Tar was used to fill in the holes in the wagon.

    H Weather was one hardship faced by the pioneers.

    J Water and firewood were sometimes hard to find.

One strategy for answering a question like this one is to skim the passages for keywords. When you look back at the passages, you can see from the information in #5 of "Mobile Home of the Pioneers" and paragraph 8 of "Trail of Courage" that the only detail that appears in both passages is that the weather was a hardship for the pioneers. Choice H is correct.

© The Continental Press, Inc.   Do not duplicate.

The organization of "Mobile Home of the Pioneers" is different from the organization of "Trail of Courage" because it

    A uses headings to show the main topics of the article

    B gives additional helpful information in call-out boxes

    C uses numbered sections to describe the parts of a wagon

    D shows words that are likely to be unfamiliar in bold print

These two articles are organized very differently. You can eliminate choices A, B, and D because these answers describe features of "Trail of Courage." Only choice C describes how "Mobile Home of the Pioneers" is organized. Choice C is the best answer.

Both passages are <u>best</u> described as which kind of writing?

    F nonfiction   **H** literary essays

    G short stories   **J** autobiographies

This question asks you to compare both passages and describe how the style of writing is similar. Choice F, nonfiction, is the only answer that fits.

Test Yourself

Read the article "It's Your Life!" Then answer Numbers 1 through 3.

It's Your Life!

There are many ways to live in the United States. People live in cities and suburbs, in trailer parks and on farms. You will have to decide how you want to live someday. You will have many choices. Will you choose to live in an apartment or a house? Will you drive a car or take buses and trains? Will you work at home or in an office? Here are two very different ways to live today.

A Simple Home

Some people live without many of the things that you use every day. In parts of the United States, Amish people live a very simple life. They live near one another and work on farms. Children walk to school. Their houses do not have electricity, and they do not drive cars or trucks. Their homes are heated with stoves, and they read by daylight or lamplight.

The Amish do not use any electronic appliances, such as vacuum cleaners or dishwashers. They sweep their floors and wash dishes and clothes by hand. They hang clothes outside to dry in the wind. Kids in the family help with all the farm and house

© The Continental Press, Inc.   Do not duplicate.

chores. Of course, there are no television sets or computers in an Amish home. People read books and newspapers and make many things. Children play with simple wooden toys.

A "Smart" Home

The word **automation** is a combination of the words **automatic** and **operation**.

Most homes today use tools and appliances that make life easier. Computers and other electronic devices control many of these machines. All these devices are examples of **"automation."** Automation makes it possible for people to do more things. Automated machines do a lot of the work that people used to do. These machines make the coffee, wash and dry the clothes, and open the garage door for us.

"Smart" homes are houses with many electronic devices that make using automated machines even easier. Remote control devices, such as the one for your TV, and keypads will mean that you don't even have to touch an appliance to make it work! You might be in your bedroom ready to go to sleep. Then you remember that you forgot to turn your computer off. All you do is punch in numbers on the keypad on your wall. The computer is turned off.

Many electronic devices are used for security. In some "smart" homes, lights turn on when someone comes to the front door. A sensor illuminates the driveway as soon as a car drives up. An alarm sounds when a window or door is broken. If a fire starts while the owners are away, an automated home will not only call the fire department, it will also alert the neighbors and even turn on the sprinklers.

sensor: n. a device that detects and responds to a signal

The light went on when I passed by the *sensor*.

Every day there are new inventions that will make life easier and safer. Someday, you will be able to give directions to your appliances with a voice command. For example, you could call your home from school and tell the oven to turn itself on to 350 degrees for 10 minutes. Or you might have a **sensor** in your mailbox. Perhaps you don't want to go out in the rain to see if there is mail. The sensor sends a signal to tell you that there is mail in the box.

Which of these devices do you think you will live with? Or will you decide on a simple life where you do things for yourself?

1 **The home of an Amish family is different from a "smart" home because an Amish family's home**

    A uses more electricity   **C** has devices with automation

    B is less work to maintain   **D** uses little modern technology

© The Continental Press, Inc.   Do not duplicate.

2 Which of these would most likely be found in a "smart" home?

F a wood stove

G a garage door opener

H a drying rack for dishes

J a tub for washing clothes

3 Which of these best describes the main difference between living a simple life and living in a "smart" home?

A Living a simple life means doing more for oneself.

B Living in a "smart" home helps people become smarter.

C Living a simple life means letting machines do the work.

D Living in a "smart" home helps people spend more time together.

Reread the draft of a student's report on page 99. Then answer Numbers 4 and 5.

4 According to the information in the report, a common reason people come to live in the United States from other countries is that they want to

F be with their families

G visit tourist attractions

H travel far from their homes

J feel like they are on vacation

5 The main difference between a citizen and an immigrant is that an immigrant has

A lived in the United States for a long time

B parents who were born in the United States

C proof of having been born in the United States

D come to the United States from another country

Read the article "Slammin' Sammy." Then answer Numbers 6 through 8.

Slammin' Sammy

The Dominican Republic is a small island country in the Caribbean Sea. It shares the island with the country of Haiti.

In the summer of 1998, the name Sammy Sosa became a household word. This twenty-nine-year-old Chicago Cubs baseball player was in the headlines of newspapers around the world. How did this young man from the Dominican Republic unexpectedly gain fame? He and St. Louis Cardinals' first baseman Mark McGwire were in a friendly competition. They both were trying to break a very old baseball record.

In 1961, the New York Yankees' Roger Maris hit a record 61 home runs in a single season. Thirty-seven years later, Sosa and McGwire finally broke Maris's record. When all was said and done, McGwire ended the regular season with 70 home runs. Sosa was not far behind with 66. Sammy Sosa did not win

Unit 4 Evaluating Text

165

© The Continental Press, Inc.   Do not duplicate.

the home run race. However, he helped his team make it to the playoffs, and he won the National League's Most Valuable Player (MVP) award. He also won the hearts of people all over the world, especially in his home country, the Dominican Republic.

Opportunity Knocks

The events of the summer of 1998 were a far cry from Sammy's childhood. As a boy in the Dominican Republic, Sammy worked hard to help his family make ends meet. When his father died, his mother was left alone to raise five boys and two girls. Sammy helped out by selling oranges, shining shoes, and washing cars. Much of the time Sammy and his friends played baseball on dirt streets. They didn't have gloves, so they would catch the ball with their hands. They often used a rolled-up sock for a ball and a stick for a bat. Sammy didn't start playing baseball on a real team until he was 14 years old.

When Sammy was just 16, baseball scouts from the United States started to notice his talent. At 17, he came to the U.S. for the first time to play ball on a minor league team. At the time, he spoke no English! Over the next few years, Sammy worked his way up in the major leagues, but he never lost sight of his family back home in the Dominican Republic. He made money to support his family. Baseball was his way to help his family.

Big Mac and Slammin' Sammy

> pressure: *n. a situation or event that causes concern*
>
> The *pressure* of having to do a report in front of the class made me nervous.

Sammy Sosa was not selfish. He learned quickly how much it meant to be part of a team. Sammy believed that his most important accomplishment in 1998 was helping his team get to the playoffs. Reporters asked Sammy about the **pressure** of the home run race with Mark McGwire. He said, "Pressure is shining shoes and washing cars to support my family in the Dominican Republic." He explained that now he went to bed happy every night and was very thankful to have the chance to play ball in the United States.

Sosa and McGwire shared the spotlight through the 1998 season. McGwire was known as "Big Mac" and Sosa was called "Slammin' Sammy." McGwire matched Roger Maris's record of 61 homers before Sosa did. However, Slammin' Sammy was not jealous. When the Cubs met the Cardinals in their final game of the season, Big Mac hit homer number 62, breaking Maris's record. Even though Sammy was chasing the same record, he ran from his position in right field to give his buddy a big hug of congratulations. It was a proud moment for Mark McGwire and St. Louis Cardinals fans.

© The Continental Press, Inc.   Do not duplicate.

A New Home

Sammy Sosa found a new home in the United States. Through baseball he has made a good life for himself and his family. But he hasn't forgotten his roots. Sammy still visits the Dominican Republic. He also helped raise money for his country after a hurricane. No wonder Sammy Sosa is beloved by two countries!

6 The <u>main</u> difference between Sammy Sosa's early life and his life in the United States is that as a child, he

    F supported his family   **H** loved to play baseball

    G struggled in poverty   **J** received special privileges

7 Sammy Sosa's reason for immigrating to the United States is <u>similar</u> to the reason many others come to this country because they

    A need to support their parents

    B have special talents and skills

    C are seeking better opportunities

    D dream of playing professional baseball

8 According to the information in the article, Sammy Sosa and Mark McGwire were alike because they <u>both</u>

    F were from the Dominican Republic

    G played on the St. Louis Cardinals team

    H had shown talent in playing baseball at a very early age

    J wanted to break a record for the most home runs in a season

Use information from all three articles to answer Numbers 9 through 11.

9 Which of these describes an idea that appears in <u>both</u> "Becoming a Citizen" and "It's Your Life!"?

    A America is the land of opportunity.

    B People must struggle to become citizens.

    C Americans are free to live as they choose.

    D Citizens have special rights and privileges.

10 Which of these describes an idea that appears in <u>both</u> "Becoming a Citizen" and "Slammin' Sammy"?

    F The United States is home to people from many countries.

    G The United States provides many opportunities to athletes.

    H Part of success is being in the right place at the right time.

    J Hard work will go far toward accomplishing one's dreams.

© The Continental Press, Inc.   Do not duplicate.

11 BCR

Write an explanation that tells one thing that someone had to give up in each article. Include details and examples from the articles to support your explanation.

Use the space below to plan your response. Then write your final draft on a separate sheet of paper.

© The Continental Press, Inc.   Do not duplicate.

Lesson 3

Evaluating Text

When you evaluate text, you make judgments about what you read. You might judge the **content** (the message or ideas), the **organization** (how the writing is put together), or the use of **language** (how the writer puts the ideas into words).

As a reader, you evaluate the content in several ways. You may evaluate the relevance, timeliness, and accuracy of the information or message of the text. Here are some questions to help you evaluate the content:

- Is the information or message of the passage significant or important? Is this passage worth reading?

- Is the information current?

- Are the facts correct?

Evaluating the organization is as simple as reading the passage and then considering how well you were able to understand what the writer was saying. Here are some questions to help you evaluate the organization:

- Does this passage make sense?

- Is the main idea clear?

- Is the main idea supported by relevant facts and details?

- Do the transitions help me move from one idea to the other?

- Is there a strong introduction and conclusion?

4.2.2 The student will explain how the specific language and expression used by the writer or speaker affects reader or listener response.

4.2.3 The student will evaluate the use of transitions and their effectiveness in a text.

As with evaluating the content and organization, evaluating the use of language means thinking about your own experience as a reader. The use of language is intended to make you think or feel a certain way.

© The Continental Press, Inc.   Do not duplicate.

When you evaluate the use of language, ask yourself:

- Is the use of language consistent?

- Is the language concise?

- Does the writer have command of the language?

- Are the words effective in helping me understand the theme or the main idea of the passage?

- Do the words create vivid images in my mind?

Guided Practice

Read the following rough draft of a report. Then answer the questions.

[1]The craft of papermaking was developed in China around 2,000 years ago. [2]The process has not changed all that much since then. [3]True, most papermaking today is done by machine, rather than by hand, as it was in the past. [4]But the machinery is pretty much the same as the obsolete process—a lot faster, to be sure. [5]Even so, many people still practice the art of making fine paper by hand, using methods very much like those of the ancient Chinese.

[6]Papermaking usually starts with wood. [7]In fact, most commercially made paper comes from trees. [8]Consequently, paper can be made from any material containing cellulose fiber. [9]Rags, sawdust, hemp, seaweed, and even grass clippings from your lawn could be made into fine stationery. [10]Many people today use recycled paper.

[11]If wood is used, the bark is stripped off and the wood is cut into small chips. [12]The machinery that is used includes digesters, beaters, and a Jordan machine. [13]The chips are placed with water and chemicals into a tank, where the chips are transformed into pulp. [14]The pulp is washed and pressed through screens before it is placed into a special tub. [15]In the tub, pressure is applied to the pulp. [16]The pressure serves two purposes: to force the water out and to make the cellulose fibers get together. [17]This creates a mat of the fibers, which is then pressed and dried. [18]The mat is now recognizable as a large, thin sheet of paper. [19]The last step is to wind the sheet into a cylinder to produce a large roll of paper.

© The Continental Press, Inc.   Do not duplicate.

Where should this sentence be placed in the rough draft?

The process is simple.

    A   between Sentences 4 and 5

    B   at the end of the second paragraph

    C   between Sentences 18 and 19

    D   at the beginning of the third paragraph

Look back at the draft. You can eliminate choices A and B because this sentence has to do with the process of making paper, which is described in detail in the third paragraph. When you read the paragraph, you can see that the sentence fits best at the beginning. Choice D is the best answer.

Which of these is the best replacement for the underlined phrase in Sentence 4?

    F   is very much like   **H**   duplicates

    G   does a similar thing as   **J**   Best as it is

Think about the way the words are used. Which answer choice is most concise? Answer choices F and G are overly wordy and too general. Choice H is the best answer.

Which of these is the best transition to replace the underlined words in Sentence 5?

    A   Similarly,   **C**   Moreover,

    B   For instance,   **D**   Best as it is

Transitions help you move from one idea to another. They show that the ideas are connected in some way. Because Sentence 5 gives a contrast to Sentence 4, the best transition is one that shows contrast. Choice A shows a comparison. Choices B and C show addition. Only choice D shows contrast, so D is the best answer.

Which of these is the best transition to replace the underlined word in Sentence 8?

    F   However,   **H**   For example,

    G   In addition,   **J**   Best as it is

Sentence 8 is also giving information in contrast to the information in Sentence 7. You can rule out choices G and H, because they show addition and example. Choice F is the best answer.

© The Continental Press, Inc.   Do not duplicate.

Which of these is the best replacement for the underlined phrase in Sentence 16?

A become connected

B cling to each other

C join and remain stuck

D Best as it is

This question asks you to evaluate the word choice. Which phrase would be most effective, most concise, and most vivid in the sentence? Choice B is the best answer.

Which sentence does not belong in the second paragraph?

F Papermaking usually starts with wood.

G In fact, most commercially made paper comes from trees.

H Rags, sawdust, hemp, seaweed, and even grass clippings from your lawn could be made into fine stationery.

J Many people today use recycled paper.

This question asks you to evaluate the organization by choosing the sentence that does not belong. The main topic of the paragraph has to do with the materials used for making paper. The sentence that is the least connected to this topic is choice J.

Which sentence does not belong in the third paragraph?

A If wood is used, the bark is stripped off and the wood is cut into small chips.

B The machinery that is used includes digesters, beaters, and a Jordan machine.

C The pulp is washed and pressed through screens before it is placed into a special tub.

D The last step is to wind the sheet into a cylinder to produce a large roll of paper.

Again, this question asks you to evaluate the organization by choosing the sentence that does not belong. The main topic of the paragraph is the process of making paper. The sentences appear in the order of the steps used for papermaking. Choice B clearly does not fit in, so choice B is the best answer.

© The Continental Press, Inc.   Do not duplicate.

Which sentence would be best to begin a fourth paragraph?

F That is how paper is made at a paper mill, but people can still make paper at home on a smaller scale.

G Hobbyists use extra-large restaurant blenders, which may be purchased at restaurant supply stores or surplus stores, to mix the pulp.

H Some of the chemicals used in making paper are toxic.

J Most people don't have a digester at home, so they use a blender.

This question is also about the organization. If you were writing a fourth paragraph, you would want to use a sentence that would help you move from the process of making paper by machine to the topic of your new paragraph. Only choice F contains information that would link the third paragraph to a new paragraph. Choice F is the best answer.

Read this poem, and answer the question that follows.

Concord Hymn

Sung at the completion of the battle monument, July 4, 1837
by Ralph Waldo Emerson

By the rude[1] bridge that arched the flood,
       Their flag to April's breeze unfurled,
Here once the embattled farmers stood
And fired the shot heard round the world.

The foe[2] long since in silence slept;
       Alike the conqueror silent sleeps;
And Time the ruined bridge has swept
Down the dark stream which seaward[3] creeps.

On this green bank, by this soft stream,
       We set to-day a votive[4] stone;
That memory may their deed redeem[5],
When, like our sires[6], our sons are gone.

Spirit, that made those heroes dare
       To die, and leave their children free,
Bid Time and Nature gently spare
The shaft[7] we raise to them and thee.

[1]rude: rough, crude, simple
[2]foe: enemy
[3]seaward: toward the ocean
[4]votive: memorial

[5]redeem: bring back
[6]sires: fathers
[7]shaft: monument stone

© The Continental Press, Inc.   Do not duplicate.

BCR Write an explanation that describes how the author's use of language in "Concord Hymn" might inspire the reader. Support your explanation with details and examples from the poem.

First, underline some of the key lines and phrases from the poem that are meant to inspire the reader. These include lines 3–4, lines 10–11, and lines 13–14. Think about the theme of this poem: "Remember the heroes." Then make some notes about how the author uses language to praise the heroes, their heroic deeds, and the monument that is being set up to memorialize them for generations to come. Lastly, use your notes to write a short response of one or two paragraphs on a separate sheet of paper.

Now read this article, and answer the question that follows.

Becoming a Citizen

Citizen—person born in the United States or born to U.S. citizens in foreign countries.

Naturalized Citizen—person born in another country who has become a citizen of the United States.

Alien—person who has come to the United States from another country.

Not everyone who lives in the United States is a citizen. People who are born in the United States are automatically citizens. But some people come to the United States from other countries. They are immigrants, or residents, but not citizens. An immigrant is a person who is allowed to live in this country without being a citizen. An immigrant must follow certain steps to become a citizen.

Why Become a Citizen?

People come to live in the United States from other countries for many reasons. Some people come to live with their family members. Others come because they can find better jobs here. Still others come because they want freedom that they do not have in their own countries.

Most people who come to the United States to live want to become citizens. Some adults want to be citizens so their children will be citizens. United States citizens have many rights and privileges. One of the most important is the right to vote. Citizens elect the president and the other people who run the government. Immigrants cannot vote. Immigrants cannot be elected to office either.

How Can an Immigrant Become a Citizen?

Suppose you have just arrived in the United States, and you want to become a citizen. The first thing you must do is

© The Continental Press, Inc.   Do not duplicate.

become a "legal permanent resident." That means you can stay here. You must live in the United States for five years as a legal permanent resident, and you must be 18 years old, before you can apply for citizenship.

You begin by filling out an application for citizenship. You must send your application to the government with your fingerprints and three pictures of yourself. Then you can take the citizenship test. This test asks questions about United States history and government. There are 20 questions, and you must get at least 12 questions right in 30 minutes. If you don't pass the test, you can take it again, as many times as you like.

> *interview: n. meeting of people face to face*
>
> I had an *interview* with the manager for my new job.

The next step is the citizenship **interview**. During the interview, a government official looks over all your papers and asks you questions. You must show in the interview that you can speak, read, and write some English. You may also have to answer more questions about U.S. government and history.

The Last Step

The last step in the process of becoming a citizen of the U.S. is taking the "Oath of Allegiance." This oath is like the Pledge of Allegiance. An "oath" or "pledge" is a promise, and "allegiance" means loyalty. When you take the oath, you promise to be loyal to the United States and not to another country. After the ceremony, a judge grants you citizenship. At last you receive a certificate that shows you are a citizen of the United States of America.

OATH OF ALLEGIANCE TO
THE UNITED STATES OF AMERICA

"I hereby declare, on oath, that I absolutely and entirely renounce and abjure all allegiance and fidelity to any foreign prince, potentate, state or sovereignty, of whom or which I have heretofore been a subject or citizen; that I will support and defend the Constitution and laws of the United States of America against all enemies, foreign and domestic; that I will bear true faith and allegiance to the same; that I will bear arms on behalf of the United States when required by the law; that I will perform noncombatant service in the armed forces of the United States when required by the law; that I will perform work of national importance under civilian direction when required by law; and that I take this obligation freely without any mental reservation or purpose of evasion; so help me God."

Unit 4 Evaluating Text

© The Continental Press, Inc.   Do not duplicate.

BCR Write an explanation that tells whether the article does or does not provide sufficient information about the process of becoming a citizen. Support your explanation with details and examples from the article.

Your first step should be to make a list of the information contained in the article about becoming a citizen. The first paragraph and the callout box beside it give definitions of all the terms: *citizen, immigrant, resident, naturalized citizen,* and *alien.* The next two paragraphs tell why people want to become citizens of the United States. Under the heading about how to become a citizen, there is a paragraph about the conditions to be met. Then three steps are outlined: 1) fill out an application, 2) take and pass a test, and 3) have a citizenship interview. Taking the "Oath of Allegiance" is the last step, found under a heading with that name.

Can you think of any information that is missing? The article does not tell about the process of becoming a citizen of a country other than the United States. Look back over the article to be sure your list and notes are complete. Then write your response on a separate sheet of paper. This one might take at least two paragraphs.

© The Continental Press, Inc.   Do not duplicate.